IS NOTHING SACRED?

BY THE AUTHOR

Keeping the Faith: Questions and Answers for the Abused Woman
Sexual Violence: The Unmentionable Sin

Is Nothing Sacred?

When Sex Invades the Pastoral Relationship

MARIE M. FORTUNE

HarperSanFrancisco

A Division of HarperCollins*Publishers*

FIRST HARPERCOLLINS PAPERBACK EDITION PUBLISHED IN 1992

Library of Congress Cataloging-in-Publication Data

Fortune, Marie M.
    Is nothing sacred? / Marie M. Fortune. — 1st HarperCollins pbk. ed.
        p. cm.
    Originally published: San Francisco : Harper & Row, c1989.
    Includes bibliographical references and index.
    ISBN 0–06–062684–4
    1. Clergy—Professional ethics—Case studies   2. Clergy—Sexual behavior—Case studies   I. Title

[BV4011.5.F67   1991]
241'.641—dc20   91–55406
                                                                                   CIP

---

92   93   94   95   96   FAIR   10   9   8   7   6   5   4   3   2   1

In loving memory of
Bernie Mitchell
who never gave up on the church

and

my grandmother
Marie Hendley Abernethy
a Methodist layleader who would have confronted
this injustice without hesitation

Contents

Acknowledgments

My deepest appreciation is extended to the women I have named in this book, Marian Murray, Joan and Barbara Preston, Kristin Stone, Katie Simpson, Bernie Mitchell, Lina Robinson, and Nancy Linder for their courage and persistence, but also for their cooperation and encouragement of me in completing this project.

I also greatly appreciate the contributions of the other principals who agreed to be interviewed, and especially of those who were willing to share their mistakes so that the church might learn from them.

In addition, I extend my sincere gratitude to the following: Anne L. Ganley, still my best critic; Ann Jones and Margaret Farley, for their careful criticism and sustaining support; Frances Goldin, for her skill in making it happen; Rebecca Laird, for her editorial support and persistence; John Robinson, for his insight and perspective; Kathy Page, for finding Henry for me; Tom and Annah Ganley, for a room with a view; Mary Wikken, for blueberry muffins; Savannah, in spite of whom the project was completed; and the Center for the Prevention of Sexual and Domestic Violence, for the sabbatical.

This is a reconstruction. All of it is a reconstruction. It's a reconstruction now, in my head, as I lie flat on my single bed rehearsing what I should or shouldn't have said, what I should or shouldn't have done, how I should have played it. . . .

It's impossible to say a thing exactly the way it was, because what you say can never be exact, you always have to leave something out, there are too many parts, sides, crosscurrents, nuances; too many gestures, which could mean this or that, too many shapes which can never be fully described, too many flavors, in the air or on the tongue, half-colors, too many. But if you happen to be a man sometime in the future, and you've made it this far, please remember: you will never be subject to the temptation of feeling you must forgive, a man, as a woman. It's difficult to resist, believe me. But remember that forgiveness too is a power. To beg for it is a power, and to withhold or bestow it is power, perhaps the greatest.

Maybe none of this is about control. Maybe it isn't really about who can own whom, who can do what to whom and get away with it . . . Maybe it isn't about who can sit and who has to kneel or stand or lie down, legs spread open. Maybe it's about who can do what to whom and be forgiven for it. Never tell me it amounts to the same thing.

MARGARET ATWOOD, *The Handmaid's Tale*

Introduction

In the middle of the nineteenth century, Henry Ward Beecher, pastor of Brooklyn's Plymouth Congregational Church for over twenty-five years, was considered by many to be "the greatest preacher since St. Paul." His biographer, Paxton Hibben, described the congregation Beecher pastored:

Plymouth Church he had created in his own image—big, prosperous, a little flamboyant, apparently self-sufficient—truculent, even—but for all that strictly a Congregational church. And when Henry Ward Beecher made his dramatic entry, flung his soft hat under a settee, wrapped his cape about him and sat looking from left to right and right to left over a sea of faces, he knew that there, in the midst of his own, he could do whatever he pleased. For these men and women who crowded pews and aisles came for certain things they could find nowhere else in an odor of sanctity: excitement, entertainment, secureness, hope, self-confidence, emotional release. These things Henry Ward Beecher gave them with all the weight of divine sanction. When he cracked his pulpit jokes, there were polite titters from the more costly pews and loud guffaws from the galleries; when he raised his voice in prayer, the tears streaming down his full cheeks, he could hear the little staccato sobs of women and the harsher sobs of men from every corner of the vast house; and when he rose to exalted flights of sonorous phrases, the applause began gently and swelled to a thunderous drumroll of triumph. Plymouth Church was a great name in the land as Henry Ward Beecher's name was great. The members of Plymouth Church were shareholders in him. He could do no wrong.[1]

In 1872, when Victoria Woodhull published allegations of Beecher's sexual liaison with Elizabeth Tilton, a member of Plymouth Church, it was not surprising that the church and the community rallied to Beecher's defense: This man was too important a church leader of the abolition and suffrage movements to be undone by such charges. The issues as presented by Woodhull were adultery and hypocrisy. She asserted that this stellar personality preached traditional Victorian morality, defending home and family from the pulpit, while carrying on an affair with a church member. His betrayal was twofold: Elizabeth Tilton was a parishioner—whom, he assured, was committing no sin with him, *and* she was also the wife of one of Beecher's closest friends, Theodore Tilton. What's more, Elizabeth Tilton was not the only object of Beecher's intimate, pastoral attentions. There had been others. Beecher called upon his other friends and associates to defend him. Even though he admitted his misconduct privately, he would not confess publicly. Faced with a suit brought by Theodore Tilton five years later, Beecher still sought to avoid admission and retain his status as the "greatest preacher in America." The power of Beecher's charisma remained unquestioned. But the events surrounding his pastoral relations and his response to allegations of misconduct revealed the essence of the man. His own words written in 1858 ironically foreshadowed his own circumstance:

Excuses for moral delinquency are, therefore, usually processes of self-deception. At first they may not be; but at length a man who tries to deceive himself comes into that state in which he can do nothing else but deceive himself. A man can put out his eyes, inwardly, so that at last he will not see that a lie is a lie, and a truth a truth. Deceit may be known to be so at first. It then becomes less and less noticeable and finally the mind is falsified and lives without frankness, openness, truth or purity. And nothing is more common than that men may be in that state, and with a certain kind of exterior morality, making them noticeably good in external matters while they have actually lost power of moral discrimination in respect to their own inward habits.[2]

Such is the case when a person who holds the public trust betrays that trust. Not only does his mind "live without frankness," but often so do the minds of many around him.

The Beecher-Tilton affair was one of the great scandals of the nineteenth century. But the scandal as it was viewed then was Beecher's disregard for Victorian morality and his hypocrisy. Questions were never raised about his professional ethics as a pastor in relation to his parishioners.

In the early 1980s, another scandal took place in an average church in an average city. Events occurred that could never happen in such a place — but they did. These events shook the foundations of the church and the faith of the many individuals whose lives were touched. They revolved around one man, the Reverend Dr. Peter Donovan, who served as pastor of the First Church of Newburg during these four years. Although he was not a figure as well known as Beecher was in his time, Donovan's persona bears a remarkable resemblance to Beecher's.

Formal complaints of professional misconduct by the pastor of the First Church of Newburg were brought by six women. The charges included sexual contact with counselees and employees, misuse of his pastoral office to coerce or manipulate parishioners, verbal threats to intimidate people who might report his activities, and the use of physical force to engage in sexual intercourse. At least three additional signed complaints and four verbal allegations were given by other church members, who were not willing to come forward publicly. There was evidence that as many as forty-five church members may have been victims of Peter Donovan.

The events that led to the complaints paint a stark picture of a minister betraying his pastoral, professional relationships. The events that followed the complaints portray another betrayal by an institution unprepared and unwilling to respond. Ultimately, the church's less than perfect ability to hear and see and act prevented this disaster from becoming a catastrophe. But the disaster was enough to cause inordinate pain for many people.

Although this is a story about a church, its pastor, and its laity, about a particular time and place and particular people, it is also a story about an institution. As such it could be a story about *any* institution. We create institutions and give them power in order to serve our needs. But the power that we give institutions can also be abused. Institutions have designated, authorized leaders who are assumed to be trustworthy, but who can and do betray that trust. Whether in schools or hospitals, courts or churches, governments or families, we assume that we can trust the people authorized, elected, or hired to carry out their duties in the best interests of the people they serve. Ordinarily we can, but sometimes we cannot.

Institutions also share a pattern of response to the misconduct of an authorized representative and to the public disclosure of that misconduct. An institution acts first on what it perceives to be its self-interest. Seldom does it identify its self-interest to be the same as the interests of the people it is supposed to serve. Thus it tries to protect itself by preventing disclosure of professional misconduct. It prefers instead to shoot the messenger, that is, to denigrate whoever had the courage to tell the secret. But protecting unethical individuals from the consequences of their unprofessional conduct ultimately undermines the credibility of the entire institution. As a result, all the designated leaders become implicitly untrustworthy and the institution becomes a sham. Eventually, the institution may realize that its interests are in fact not served by avoidance, but by facing the reality that some very few of its leaders are untrustworthy and dangerous and should be removed from their professional roles. The institution has the power and responsibility to protect the people it is called to serve, thereby safeguarding its own credibility. Once it accepts this responsibility, it has the capacity to name the evil in its midst and to act justly in order to rectify harm done.

This is also a story about a community of faithful people bound together over many years by personal faith, tradition, and shared experience. For its members, the church is a spiritual home, a place where they struggle with questions and answers of ultimate importance in their lives. It is a gathering of people who share their spiritual journeys and passages, celebrate life and mourn death. It is a place where they seek to know God in their midst and to live their lives accordingly.

It is a story about the church as family. The familial model of church life has developed in recent years in an effort to overcome the isolation of contemporary life and to build intimate, caring relationships among church members. Unfortunately, just as there is potential for abuse in families, there is potential for abuse in the church that views itself as family. In this case, the abuse was sexual and the church reacted much like family members to the revelation of incest.

This is the story of a church as an institution, as a community of faith, and as a family. It is the story of a pastor, Dr. Peter Donovan; of six women, who risked a great deal to come forward and tell the secrets of their relationships with him; of the many players who knew and did nothing, or who knew and did something; and of a congregation which was broken apart by the actions of its pastor. It is a story about ordinary, decent, well-meaning people faced with extraordinary circumstances.

I was called in the late spring of 1984 to serve as an advocate and pastor for the women who came forward to make formal complaints. I was asked to help because I am an ordained minister and the executive director of the Center for the Prevention of Sexual and Domestic Violence. During the next three months, I met with the women on a number of occasions. I listened to their painful stories over potluck suppers. I strategized with them about their options over coffee. I consulted by phone. I helped them prepare their formal statements of complaint. I prayed with them. I shared their anger and frustration, their hope and despair, their intense longing for justice from their church.

My role was not simple. Frequently, I was torn between my strong commitment to the women, fueled by my anger at what had been done to them, and my love for the church and my hope that it would do its best to rectify this situation. I wanted the system to work *for* them, to make justice out of injustice, and I believed that the church had the capacity to do this. But I was constantly aware that my task was to stand by the women and, as necessary, against the church; my task was not to try to save the church from itself. This position was consistent with my theology, that is, standing by those who are powerless and vulnerable in the face of the power of institutions. It is fundamental to Hebrew and Christian teachings. The Hebrew prophets took the side of the downtrodden and oppressed over against the powers and principalities; the Gospels lifted up those vulnerable to harm at the hands of others. Justice is always the goal.

Although I expected the church also to act from these motivations, I was constantly aware that the church, like all institutions, carries a mentality of institutional self-protection. Hence I was disappointed along the way when the church's institutional values displaced its theological ones; but I was never surprised.

I was continually amazed and inspired by the faith of the women. Each had been deeply betrayed by someone whom she trusted implicitly, someone who represented both the church and God. Yet these women still expected the church to right the wrong that was done to them, to be true to its values and rhetoric. They were still willing to engage in a process they believed would vindicate them. They did not simply walk away. Throughout the process they remained at risk for further harm, they were vilified publicly and privately, and yet they persevered. Their enormous courage, their care for each other, their righteous anger, and their love of the church were for me the incarnation of the Gospel. They kept me going when I despaired that we would ever get anywhere.

The purpose of this book is to answer two major questions. The first: Was this journey really necessary? The answer is no. This situation could have been prevented. The second: What was finally accomplished? Dr. Peter Donovan is no longer pastor of First Church of Newburg and will never be able to be a minister in that denomination again. The church leaders faced some hard realities about themselves and made some changes in the way they do business. Five women survived, and this was no small accomplishment. One, whose cancer had long been in remission, had a recurrence and died in early 1986. Unfortunately, the women never felt vindicated. At best, they received only approximate justice. They deserved more than they got. But if they lost the battle, they won the war. They called the institutional church to account. Their story and the lessons they have to teach us mean that the church can never again pass by on the other side, pretending that things like this cannot happen here.

I will tell this story as truthfully and carefully as I can. I will tell it from the perspective of the women, because when considering the question of whose perspective should be taken as definitive in an ethical situation, "the one against whom power is used has the more accurate perspective on the situation."[3] I will tell the story in great detail, because the particulars of the women's experiences and of the actions in response to them are important. They reveal an institution totally unprepared and initially unwilling to protect its people from the actions of one of its designated leaders.

The situation that arose at First Church of Newburg is in some ways an extreme instance of betrayal of the pastoral relationship. But it is extreme only in terms of the severity of the pastor's assaultive and abusive behavior. It is not extreme in terms of the situations he exploited, the methods he employed, the numbers of people he harmed, or the resistance of the church to knowing the truth. In regard to the dynamics that allowed for such behavior, it is a typical case. I chose it (from nearly fifty others with which I have had some association) to illustrate the problem of professional misconduct by a pastor, because it carries within it virtually every aspect of the issue and of the difficulty of the church's response. It may strike you as so extreme as to be unbelievable. Some of the events *were* unbelievable; but this does not mean that they are not true. You may conclude that this case is so extreme that it must be an isolated incident; these things simply do not happen in the church. Unfortunately, instances of pastoral misconduct are far more common than any of us would like to believe. They may not be as far-reaching or as extreme as in the Newburg situation, but the damage to individuals and to the church is often just as serious.

I offer this story in the hope that what First Church learned from the experience of a very painful four years will encourage churches to prepare themselves to deal fairly, quickly, and effectively with instances of pastoral misconduct that are brought into the open. Other institutions face similar situations of professional misconduct; forethought and preparation will also serve them well. These situations are instances of secrecy yearning for truth-telling, of brokenness longing for healing, of injustice crying out for justice. The church has a choice when faced with such occurrences: It can turn a deaf ear, or it can heed the call of its own theology to attend to the powerless who are victims of its own power. It can keep faith with itself and its people. It can seek to do justice as a means to healing and restoration for all concerned. It can preserve the sacred trust that rests within the pastoral relationship.

1. The First Church of Newburg

Finally, brothers and sisters, whatever is true, whatever is honorable, whatever is just, whatever is pure, whatever is lovely, whatever is gracious, if there is any excellence, if there is anything worthy of praise, think about these things. What you have learned and received and heard and seen in me, do; and the God of peace will be with you.

PHILIPPIANS 4:8–9

Newburg is a city of 55,000 people just north of a large metropolitan area somewhere in the United States. A large manufacturing plant nearby employs a number of its residents. Mostly white and middle-class, essentially conservative and primarily Republican, it likes to see itself as a stable, family-oriented community. It is the county seat and was originally a small city unto itself, with its own industry and a strong economic base. Newburg became a bedroom community in two waves. First came the postwar, early stages of suburbanization in the fifties. The dream of the perfect, white-picket-fenced, nuclear family readily took root here. Then, in the seventies, the second wave began: The advent of high-tech industry in the region and the slow but persistent approach of urban sprawl turned Newburg into the ideal suburb. People who could, preferred to live here rather than in the big city. They believed that here they could avoid the problems they read about in *Newsweek*: drugs, teen pregnancy, racial unrest, gays, violence, and the sexual revolution.

By the early eighties, people who had lived in Newburg all their lives had raised their families and were moving into retirement homes or dying off. This left room for new residents to move in, young couples with young children, the next generation of suburbanites. Newburg was a livable city, an all-American city, a place to raise a family. Here the Garden Club planted flowers along the boulevard, the Lions Club held its annual auction to raise money for scholarships, the Catholic Youth Organization held a car wash at least once every summer, and families sent four-page mimeographed letters to relatives at Christmas. In the minds of its citizens, Newburg did not have a reputation of a fast and loose, situation-ethics lifestyle as did its somewhat notorious big city neighbor to the south. This is why they lived here and not there. They were looking for conventionality to be a shelter against the storm of the sexual revolution raging around them. They believed they had found it in Newburg. And many looked to the church to be the rock of their salvation, their anchor in the storm.

One such church was the First Church of Newburg, an old, established church affiliated with a mainline Protestant denomination. Today it remains, chastened by the events described here, but still living out its mission to the people of Newburg. It is conventional but not stuffy, trying to maintain tradition and be contemporary at the same time. Its members are good Christian people who mean well, who give a lot to their church, and who care about each other and their community. Appearances matter to the people there, sometimes at the expense of other things. Tight smiles may hide the pain of secrets deemed shameful, such as alcoholism or wife abuse. They see the church as different from other institutions. They believe it is a refuge from a sordid world, a place where one assumes civility and morality, a place engaged in the world but not susceptible to the same worldly realities of other institutions. Like most other churches, it does not deal well with conflict. Its banner might well read: "Jesus Christ is Lord" and in small print underneath: "If you can't say something nice about someone, then don't say anything at all." Problems tend not to be dealt with *in* church, but are surely talked about in the parking lot *after* church.

The members of First Church are not pietistic, but they take their religion seriously. They are intelligent and mature in their understanding of God and the faith. This theological sophistication is the result of some solid religious education along the way. They are by no means Bible-thumpers, but they do expect their pastor's theology to be sound and rooted in scripture. They want substance from their preacher. They trust their pastor implicitly with the most important parts of their lives, but they are also as susceptible as any-one else to the hook of personal charisma: the winning smile; the sincere, intense eye contact; the warm, caring hug.

The original First Church of Newburg was built over a hundred years ago across from city hall. By the middle of the twentieth century, this church was paying attention to its sociological milieu. In the mid-fifties, First Church abandoned its building in the center of town and moved out into the new subdivision. It was the first mainline Protestant church in the area to make this "visionary relocation," as it was called then. It was moving to be where the people were. Not unlike many churches of that era, its priority was to grow, to bring young families into its membership. And its success was noteworthy. During those years, a dynamic pastor led the congregation. The new church was built, the budget was fully pledged, the membership increased. At one point, the participation of as many as 150 young people made it necessary to hire a youth pastor. This period of about ten years came to be remembered as the Golden Era of First Church. Church leaders were proud of these accomplishments which were, both in their eyes and the eyes of their denomination, measures of real success.

First Church of Newburg became known in the District[1] as a trend-setter, a successful model of church growth for the late fifties. Leaders from First Church became leaders in the District. The relationship was clearly one of mutual benefit. The District had no regrets that it had lent First Church the money to build its new building. The investment was paying off well. And, as they would discover in the future, the return would be even greater than they had anticipated.

For the next ten years or so, life at First Church was predictable and ordinary. It became an establishment church in Newburg. Membership there carried prestige. For some, this was a means of upward mobility; for others, a symbol of an accomplished fact. Members included teachers, local government officials, corporate middle managers, retired military officers, homemakers, contractors, and business people. Most of the women worked in the home, most of the men in the workplace. But the early seventies brought a decline in membership and activity that was common throughout mainline churches. The membership was aging and fewer young families were to be seen. Church growth ground to a halt. The Golden Era was but a memory of the pillars of First Church.

The last senior minister left First Church in 1978. When a pastor leaves a church of this denomination, the church hires a new minister through a selection process that may take as long as a year. During this period, an interim minister was hired to perform the basic pastoral duties. A search committee was appointed to carry out the process of selecting a new pastor. Résumés had to be received from the District; interviews needed to be held; references had to be checked.

This time the sometimes arduous but important process of selecting a pastor was carried out by the search committee, which was made up mostly of men and experienced church leaders. There was first one interim pastor and then another as the process dragged on. The search committee began to get pressure from the members to complete their work. It had been fifteen months since they had had a senior minister.

The committee had gone about its work carefully and its members were as eager as anyone else to hire a new person. But they had not found a candidate with whom they were pleased, so they kept looking. Late in the process they received a résumé from the District office for the Reverend Dr. Peter Donovan. The professional, typeset résumé immediately caught their attention. It looked good; he looked good. He quickly rose to the top of the pile and became one of the three final candidates.

Dr. Pete Donovan presented impeccable credentials, which included a Masters of Divinity from one Ivy League seminary and a Doctor of Ministry from another. His extensive résumé revealed great skills as an administrator, counselor, and preacher. The churches he had served had grown impressively during his tenure. The fact that Donovan was previously married, divorced, and now single did not raise an eyebrow on the committee. The denomination's teaching about divorce was relatively liberal, and this church was painfully familiar with divorce. A previous staff member had divorced during his time of service there. They passed quickly over this familiar fact of life, but they did inquire as to his current relational status. He told them that he was engaged to a medical student who was still living in the area he had just left; the woman appeared later, was introduced to the search committee, and was never mentioned again.

As is commonly the practice, one of the committee members was dispatched to Donovan's previous church to take a look. There he found a big, successful looking congregation whose members seemed to regard Donovan highly. There was just one small thing. In conversation, one woman from the congregation began to tell the committee member about a problem that had arisen during Dr. Donovan's tenure. She was abruptly stopped by another member, who simply said, "We don't talk about that." Upon his return, the member reported this incident to the committee. He added that he had felt a vague sense of disquiet when he visited Donovan in his home; he was no more specific than that. But when the committee checked with the references Donovan gave from this church, they received only glowing reports. The perfunctory check of his denominational references revealed nothing that might give a committee pause. His presence in the initial interview fit his paper credentials. He impressed the committee as a bright, self-assured, powerful individual whose charisma was instantly infectious. They began to refer to him as their "knight on a white horse" who could take them back to the Golden Era of the First Church. According to one member of the committee, he seemed almost too good to be true.

Feeling pressured and frustrated, the committee was eager to be done with its job. The members of First Church had prayed and longed for a strong pastor who could help them grow again, as new young families moved into their neighborhoods. Believing that their prayers had been answered, First Church of Newburg enthusiastically called Pete Donovan to be their pastor. He was handsome, single, and thirty-six years old.

2. The Reverend Dr. Peter Donovan

But you rise against my people as an enemy; you strip the robe from the peaceful, from those who pass by trustingly . . . The women of my people you drive out from their pleasant houses . . . Arise and go, for this is no place to rest; because of uncleanness that destroys with a grievous destruction. If a man should go about and utter wind and lies, saying "I will preach to you of wine and strong drink," he would be the preacher for this people!

MICAH 2:8–11

"You're the worst kind of sinner, Joe Deets. You are the kind who think there is no such a thing as sin. You think that the only sin is getting caught."

JOHN D. MACDONALD, *One More Sunday*

Peter Donovan was just what First Church was looking for. Unconsciously, the search committee and the congregation were functioning under the pendulum principle of hiring a pastor. According to the principle, a church will replace a previous pastor, good or bad, with someone entirely different. In this case, they went from someone who was stable to the point of boredom to Pete Donovan, who was young, flashy, and dynamic. He was, in a word, impressive, and they were impressed. He projected an Eagle Scout image of idealism and ambition. He was exciting and he was smooth. He did not appear crass; he did not insult their intelligence; he was not simplistic. He had a style they liked. His theology was part "human potential" and part "power of positive thinking" mixed with occasional scripture. A latter-day Norman Vincent Peale, he was upbeat and energizing. He believed that with love and encouragement the church could do marvelous things. In every way, he appeared to be a stimulating, competent professional. Although they did not use the word until later to describe him, he was charismatic; his personal magnetism aroused intense loyalty in many people.

Upon his arrival at First Church, Donovan immediately set about to get to know the nearly 500 members and began to put his stamp on the organizational structures of the church. His preaching was exciting and dynamic and instantly attracted new members to First Church. Donovan moved quickly to get these new members into key positions in the church. This was good news all around. The pillars of the church were delighted to have fresh, young people take on some of the nitty-gritty jobs they had so long carried. They occasionally realized that they were no longer in charge or even in touch with the inner workings of the church, but they did not mind a bit. Instead they were relieved and delighted with the changes Pete Donovan brought. He was friendly and approachable; he gave them personal attention and appeared to care for each of them. Only later would their naive assessment of him come back to haunt them.

It was not difficult for Donovan to recruit volunteers to help with a variety of new programs. Soon his staff, in addition to a paid secretary, was made up of seven program coordinators, all of whom were laywomen. A creative administrator, he delegated responsibility and authority well. He elicited strong loyalties from those around him. Even though they were volunteers, the program coordinators were eager to work long hours to assist Donovan in any way possible with his ministry. First Church was flourishing under his leadership. New members were recruited mostly by staff members. The program expanded to include an after-school children's program, a singles ministry, an outreach program to one of the local tourist attractions, a cassette tape ministry using Donovan's sermons, and many more. All of the church's promotional materials were now professionally typeset and printed instead of mimeographed. And the focus of each piece was Pete Donovan. Donovan recruited people to *him*. He elicited commitments to himself, not to the church. Many of the newcomers were more fans of Pete Donovan than members of First Church. In the crunch, their loyalty would shape their actions.

He did not hesitate to let it be known to his colleagues that he used to teach preaching at a prestigious seminary, that his membership was increasing by leaps and bounds,[1] that his media ministry program was really taking off, and that he had great plans for First Church. Although he could play good-old-boy with the best, he tended not to associate with the other pastors in the denomination. He was essentially a lone ranger. When approached by clergy colleagues and invited to events, he would reply that he was too busy. He never seemed to have problems or questions or hesitations to share with a fellow pastor. Collegiality was not on his agenda. In spite of this, Donovan quickly became known throughout the District of the denomination as a forceful, vibrant, ambitious, and effective pastor. His successful appearance convinced the District that he was someone to watch, and overcame their initial discomfort with his lack of collegiality. What they did not realize was that Donovan was carefully keeping his distance from the District and the denomination. For example, he studiously avoided using denominational designations on promotional materials or in reference to First Church. He had plans for First Church that did not include the denomination.

Within the congregation, his solitary style was also apparent. He was such a private person that he allowed only a few members to know his personal phone number or where he lived. He was accessible only through the church secretary and several other laywomen. If members had an emergency and needed Dr. Donovan's attention at the hospital, they had to reach him through one of these people. Even the president of First Church did not have direct access to him. Some members felt this was unusual, but at the same time they knew Donovan was very busy; they appreciated the importance of the pastor's privacy and wanted to respect it. It did not occur to them until much later that Donovan was not protecting his privacy as much as he was his secrets.

There was no question that Donovan was a great communicator. In Sunday worship, he spoke eloquently, without notes, moving freely across the front of the sanctuary in a flowing black clerical robe. People came expecting to get something they could take away and they always thought they did. But after a while, some realized they were not getting so much after all. Thoughtful people in the congregation began to have to look for Donovan's theology. He seemed almost apologetic for using scripture. His sermons were more gimmick than Gospel, more surface than substance. When he would baptize an infant, he would carry the child around the sanctuary, presenting it to the congregation, and then expound on the fact that the water he was using was that which he had taken from the river Jordan on his last visit to the Holy Land, the same water used to baptize Jesus. The point of this exposition was not the meaning of the rite of baptism and the importance of this child, but the importance of Pete Donovan, who frequented Israel and brought back this special water just for First Church. The theatrics always turned the focus on him, and for a while they played well to the audience. But over the months, Donovan's preaching wore thin, especially for some of the old-timers. They expected more than the theological shallowness and superficiality they were getting. But rather than voice a concern or raise an objection, they simply stayed away.

As a pastor, Donovan was very present to the members. Whenever someone was ill or in mourning, in need of reassurance or guidance, he was there. He gave personal attention to every member and seemed able to connect to individuals in a very immediate and intimate way. But he also had a way of making people feel indebted to him for all he did for them. He made sure they realized that he had gone out of his way to be with them. Nothing was ever freely given; he expected their unconditional loyalty in return. He used the intimacy of his pastoral relationship to manipulate them, always reminding them how special they were to him. Later they would discover that when this did not suffice, he used his anger and the threat of physical violence to intimidate and control. In meetings, he would pound on the table while his face turned purple with rage.

Many church members learned early that it was a waste of time to approach Donovan, to challenge or question him. He made it clear to everyone that this was *his* church and if they did not like the way he ran it, they could go somewhere else. He did not allow anyone to question his actions.

The only obstacle to Donovan's ambitious plans for First Church was the lack of money to fund all the programs he wanted. Donovan was especially insistent on expanding his media and tape ministry, a self-promotion scheme that would expand his popularity and power base beyond First Church. By and large, the congregation saw this as an outreach ministry, a way to reach people not ordinarily touched by the church, and they supported the idea.

At the same time, Donovan was pushing to have First Church pay off its mortgage loans to the District, because he knew that the mortgage meant that the denomination in fact owned First Church's building and property. A few of the pillars became uncomfortable with Donovan's eagerness to minimize any hold the denomination might have over the church. These were people committed and loyal to the denomination long before Donovan ever appeared on the scene. They had long-standing relationships with members of the denomination outside First Church with whom they had shared many common projects. Earlier they had objected to the lack of denominational designation on promotional materials for First Church. Now they were very hesitant to pay off the loans. They did not take lightly what could be the beginning of the end of their relationship to the denomination. But rather than raise the issue head on and run the risk of being labeled paranoid and uncooperative, they presented Donovan with a choice: There was enough money either to support his media ministry or pay off the denomination. He would simply have to choose. He chose the media ministry. The mortgage was retained by the District. In the months ahead, this would prove to be an important hedge against Donovan's efforts to pull First Church entirely out of its denomination.

Dr. Donovan's rapidly developing reputation was not limited to his professional skills. Rumors began to fly about his being a womanizer. Donovan and many members of First Church who heard such things dismissed them. He was a divorced, single, attractive man who was also a public figure, and thus was likely to encounter such rumors. It was simply one of the liabilities of the job.

But by the late spring of 1984, in the fourth year of Donovan's tenure at First Church, there were more than just rumors. Complaints had been made to the District office and formal charges of "conduct unbecoming the ministry" and "moral turpitude" were being prepared. Faced with the fact that his secrets were no longer secret, Donovan decided to play hard ball and to play it fast. He threatened to pull First Church out of the denomination, believing that he had sufficient support from the membership. But the old-timers of First Church never allowed it. When this strategy eluded him, Donovan took steps to cover his flanks. His biggest fear was public disclosure of his activities. Once he realized he would have to leave First Church, he tried to cover up the real reasons. In the end, he voluntarily resigned and gave up his standing[2] as a minister in his denomination on the condition that there be no public hearing of the charges nor official disclosure of the substance of the charges. The steps that led to this final action reveal a great deal about the man, Peter Donovan, and about the church he served.

3. The Women's Stories

It's always been like a hunt. The right wind direction, camouflage, weaponry. All the right words. Walk lightly and move ever closer. Never be hasty. Never give up. It's been my avocation. And once they are caught, and when finally the novelty is gone, and the loving is getting too familiar, then I shuck them, as gently as possible, leaving as few scars as I can. And I've always been able to justify it by twisting the facts around. Doreen had been treated badly by her dead motorcycle friend. So-and-so's husband has been neglecting her shamefully. What's-her-name has never realized how attractive she is and it needs to be proven to her. . . .

Oh no, he thought. You talk about wickedness and contemplate this act. And even as you contemplate it, you are telling yourself, in a kindly tone, like an uncle, that this would be an absolutely certain way of sealing her lips. She's been readied by all the talk, by all the churn of emotions, by her own fears and uncertainties. In a matter of minutes it could begin, and all her protestations would be listless, her voice small, her body slack with only token resistance. . . .

JOHN D. MACDONALD, *One More Sunday*

I received a call at my office from Rev. Ralph Bennett, the associate District minister, in late June 1984. I knew Bennett through mutual friends, but had never worked with him. He knew of my work with the Center for the Prevention of Sexual and Domestic Violence. He said that the District was dealing with a very messy case of pastoral abuse and he knew that I had experience with such cases in the church. Would I be willing to come and meet with the women who were bringing complaints and be their advocate? I immediately said yes. Although I had served both as consultant to church committees on this issue and been an informal supporter of a number of individual victims, I had never had the opportunity to serve in the advocacy role at the behest of the church and at this stage of the process. I knew I had something to offer, and I was also challenged by what I would learn.

On July 16, 1984, I flew into the regional airport and Bennett picked me up. The women were expecting me for supper at one of their homes. Bennett filled me in on the particulars of what had been done thus far. We drove to the house where we would meet; I did not know what to expect and I am certain that the women did not either. Five of the six women were there. The sixth was out of town, but we were meeting in her mother's home and she more than adequately represented her daughter's concerns. We sat down and they introduced themselves: Marian, Kristin, Barbara, Katie, Bernie, and Nancy. I knew nothing about their individual experiences except that they were the women who were prepared to make formal complaints about the conduct of their pastor. I also knew that the charges were serious and that there was already some evidence that there were more than these six victims.

I have talked with many victims of different forms of abuse and I have seen them act in myriad ways. Some victims are very controlled, others very anxious, others flippant; some victims are visibly depressed and immobilized, others angry; occasionally some are a little flakey, some clearly have mental disorders. I expected to see all of these states among these six women.

Instead I found six intent, angry women who might well have been a bridge club. They were the female essence of a white middle-class suburb. Their ages ranged from twenty-four to sixty-five, their appearances from stereotypically attractive to ordinary. Any one could have been a member of my family. I was amazed to discover that they had known each other prior to this only in pairs—two here, another two there—through their activities at First Church, and then only casually. Since they had begun to meet together several weeks before, they had become more than they could ever have been alone. They had heard each other's stories in embarrassing detail. They discovered that their lives had overlapped in ways they did not even know. They had cried and grieved. They knew they were no longer alone with the secret they had carried for months. Together they discovered their rage at what had been done to them and at what had not been done to stop Peter Donovan. Any hesitation they had before meeting each other had evaporated. Together they were determined to do something about this situation.

If they were easy and comfortable with each other, they were anything but that with me. Their gracious distance with me was not surprising. Why should they be otherwise? Who was I to them except someone else representing the church, the clergy? I suppose I naively assumed that my being a woman would cut across all of that and that they would readily welcome me in their midst. It was not that easy. How did they know that I was not someone sent by the District to assess their credibility and stability, to determine if they were telling the truth or were just crazy? How did they know that I would not be watching out for the interests of the District rather than theirs? They had said that they wanted me to come, but it was clear to me that I had to prove myself to them if I was to gain their trust.

That first night I mostly listened, and I believed what I heard. As each woman described her experience, the stories rang true and a familiar pattern quickly emerged. My main concern was to get as full a picture as possible of their experiences and to assess how they were doing at this stage. I had some idea of what lay ahead for them and I was concerned about how they would hold up. Given all they had been through in the past two years, individually they were functioning surprisingly well. None of them was flakey, depressed or in need of therapy. They needed support and information. They were healthy survivors, at times anxious or discouraged about what lay before them, but generally energized by a healthy anger to move ahead.

Never did they speak of vengeance or spitefulness. Consistently their shared concern was for the other women whom they knew had also been victims, and for those who might yet become victims of Donovan. This was not so much out of their magnanimous altruism as it was for them the most concrete and immediate thing upon which they could focus: They did not want anyone else to suffer as they had.

I tried to talk about my background and experience. I brought a copy of my book *Sexual Violence: The Unmentionable Sin*, thinking that someone might find it useful. One of them took it home. I talked about the similar cases with which I had had some contact. I talked about how I saw these situations, what the issues were, and in general what I thought needed to be done about it. But I knew that all of my credentials and high-minded words were not really important to them. They had been taken in before by these things. They were interested in something much less tangible and they were going to reserve judgment on me for a while.

I asked questions to clarify the details, but was careful not to question the essence of their telling. The scope and the extremity of Donovan's behavior unnerved me. In this sense, this situation was far more serious and more urgent than I had anticipated. This man was not merely a nuisance, he was dangerous. And the fact that he still had free rein and access to this community of people was unconscionable.

These are the women's stories as they unfolded that night and more fully in the weeks to come.

Joan Preston

Joan Preston had been a member of First Church from childhood. She had been active as a teenager in church programs. In early 1980, at age twenty-one, she was living and working in Toronto, but maintained her church membership at First Church and attended whenever she was home visiting her family.

In April 1980, Joan's father died. Dr. Peter Donovan, recently installed pastor of First Church, officiated at her father's memorial service. Joan remained in Newburg for two weeks to be with her family. During this period, Donovan initiated a dating relationship with Joan. She was very attracted to this eligible bachelor. He was ruggedly handsome, bright, charming, and a minister. This combination was considered quite a catch in Newburg. Joan's mother, Barbara, was delighted.

Barbara Preston was active and well-regarded in First Church and in the District. Chairperson of the First Church stewardship board, she was a significant player in the congregation. Barbara was initially impressed by Donovan. She liked what she thought to be his gifts for ministry and the direction he wanted to lead the church, so she was pleased that her daughter was involved with the minister. In the beginning, Joan seemed to be very happy. Later, when she had doubts about Donovan, she felt reassured because of her mother's position in the church. She assumed that Donovan would not attempt to manipulate or deceive her, since her mother was in a position of some authority and status in First Church. But as this relationship developed and Barbara began to observe Donovan more closely, she became concerned.

After Joan returned to Toronto, she continued her relationship with Donovan by phone. Whenever she was in Newburg, any time she and Donovan spent together—including their sexual activity—was at the Preston home. They seldom went out in public.

Initially, Joan consented to the sexual intimacy Donovan initiated. But she began to feel uncomfortable because their relationship was primarily sexual. Furthermore, they were only sexual at her mother's home while her mother was away, or kissing and petting in Donovan's church office five minutes before the Sunday service was to begin. He never acknowledged their relationship in public. Preston began to express some dissatisfaction with this arrangement: She did not like the secrecy and the fact that they always had to worry about getting caught. Donovan countered her and said that almost "getting caught" made sex more exciting for him.

Their relationship continued for a year and a half. Joan moved back to Newburg, and she and Donovan began to discuss marriage. During this time, Donovan continually stressed the importance of secrecy. Joan was to tell no one about their relationship. He also swore her family to secrecy. Everyone willingly agreed to this request. They believed that the couple deserved as much privacy as possible. But Donovan's demand for secrecy began to raise questions about the merits of this relationship.

Other experiences raised more questions. Several times a week, Donovan would telephone after 2 A.M. wanting to talk with Joan. In the course of these calls, he would swear at her, and use abusive language about her and other members of First Church. He would also speak in sexually graphic terms to her, describing his fantasies and desires for her. Preston began to feel as if she were talking with an obscene caller. Her mother, Barbara, overheard some of these calls and saw the impact they had on Joan. The late-night phone calls, the yelling and screaming, and the cursing of church members started to unnerve Barbara. She became very apprehensive about the relationship her minister was having with her daughter.

In the summer of 1981, over a year into their relationship, Joan went to a church dinner. While there, she noticed that Donovan was sitting with another young woman from the church, Jackie Randell. Joan was surprised, beause she had expected that he would be sitting with her. She sat at another table, where she overheard an interesting conversation: Jackie Randall must be the woman Donovan was going to marry, because he was over at her house nearly every night. Joan was shocked and left the dinner immediately. When she got home, her hurt and anger poured out. All she knew was that the man whom she had been dating for over a year and was planning to marry was seeing another woman. She was devastated by what she thought was his duplicity and rejection of her. What she did not know was that there was more than one "other woman."

Hurt but silent, Joan continued to see him. During the next month, she started to hear things about other women who were involved with Donovan. She began to realize that this was not a personal affront to her, but a pattern of manipulative behavior on his part. She was just another object, one of many. In September, Joan was approached by one of the "other women," Marian Murray. They compared notes on their respective relationships with Donovan: the lines he used, the phone calls, the outbursts of anger. Joan became convinced that she wanted nothing more to do with Pete Donovan and told him so.

Five months later, Donovan called Joan and asked her out to lunch. She wasn't as furious as she had been, but she was certainly still angry enough to be cautious. She was surprised by his call, but also curious at what he could possibly want. She agreed to meet him for lunch. The lunch conversation turned out to be inconsequential and superficial. As they prepared to part in the parking lot, Joan said to Donovan that she would appreciate it if he would stop telling people that she had been after him for months, because their relationship was totally finished. He turned to her with a look of total amazement and said, "What do you mean? I am still in love with you." Joan told him that she knew he was sleeping with a lot of women from First Church, and that while she really did not care about that anymore, he should know that he was ruining his career. She advised him: "Maybe you ought to choose between this lifestyle and the ministry: you can't have both." Again in amazement, he replied, "But the ministry is my life." Joan further suggested that he find someone he really cared about instead of continuing these indiscriminate affairs. Her advice apparently was wasted on Peter Donovan.

The next Sunday, Joan attended church and Donovan approached her. He said he had taken her advice and found someone he thought he would marry. She replied that she was pleased for him and wished him well. Then he told her that *she* was the one for him. Appalled, Joan replied, "No way; I'm not interested; and I think you are full of it." He did not call her again. Taking note of the painful lessons she had learned, Joan resolved to get on with her life.

Marian Murray

Marian Murray moved to Newburg with her husband and children in the late fifties and joined First Church. She taught Sunday school when her children were young and attended worship services regularly. Her husband served on the stewardship board and as a deacon. First Church was important to her, but the main focus of her activity was the community. She was widely known and respected in Newburg and served on the Human Services Commission beginning in 1974. When Dr. Peter Donovan was called to First Church, Murray was enthusiastic about his future ministry with their congregation. He clearly brought gifts which would be of great benefit to the congregation. He seemed concerned about community problems and Murray had long wanted her church to be more involved in the community.

Murray's husband died in late 1979, and the next months were not an easy transition for her. Nearly a year later, Pete Donovan officiated at her niece's wedding. Knowing that this had been a difficult year for Murray's family, Donovan was very sensitive and solicitous as he assisted with the marriage. Murray appreciated his attention, and this personal experience of Donovan's pastoral skills confirmed her belief that First Church had been fortunate in its selection of a new pastor.

In early December, Murray contacted Donovan to ask his help with one of her children, who was having difficulty adjusting to his father's death. Donovan was eager to help and came to her home on December 17, 1980, to counsel with her. They discussed her child's difficulties, and Donovan gave her a warm and reassuring hug when he left. Murray felt comforted and certain that Donovan would be able to help her child.

Peter Donovan seemed to be conscientious in his pastoral care: He stopped by in the evening to see Murray again on December 23 and 31. Each time he visited briefly, said goodbye to Murray's children, and went out to start his car. Murray walked with him. On these occasions, his warm hugs turned to passionate kisses; he told Murray that she "was the only woman for me." Murray was surprised yet flattered by his attentions and responsive to his embraces. Yet she was also confused. She had sought his counsel to help her deal with her child's problems; she needed direction and support in order to help her child. But she thought that perhaps Pete Donovan knew better than she what she needed. Perhaps she did need care and affection for herself too, which he could best provide.

Murray heard from Donovan again less than a week later on January 4, 1981. He called and suggested that they meet and talk. She eagerly accepted and looked forward to some time together. Once again she found him charming and easy to be with. He suggested they go to his home for coffee. Immediately after arriving there, Donovan told Murray that he wanted to go to bed with her. Again she felt surprised but flattered. She hesitated as she thought of her husband, who had been dead just over a year. She had not even dated another man since his death. Was her pastor's suggestion appropriate? Was it ethical? Was it right for her? She realized that she had missed the emotional and sexual intimacy she had shared with her husband, and she longed to have that again. Murray shared her hesitation and questions with Donovan. He was her pastor and she trusted and respected him. As she wavered, Donovan reassured her: It was perfectly acceptable; she should know that he would not suggest anything that was not for her well-being.

Murray's sadness and longing, which she had held in for the past year, poured out. Finally, here was someone who cared deeply for her and who could respond to her just as she had cared for all the other family members during the past year. Perhaps it was possible to meet her needs, too. After all, they were both single, mature adults. Murray consented to have sex with Pete Donovan; this was the voice of her loneliness and vulnerability speaking.

Once Donovan's relationship with Murray became sexual, he told her that it was to be secret and that she should tell no one about it. Murray willingly agreed to this request, because she still felt confused and ambivalent; she was embarrassed to share her experience with any of her friends. But this also meant that she had no one except Donovan with whom to sort through her feelings and questions.

Murray met Donovan on two more occasions in January. Both included sexual intercourse. Murray remained ambivalent about the relationship. On the one hand, she enjoyed the affection and apparent intimacy; on the other, she wondered if this complication was what she needed in her life.

Early in February, Murray had lunch with a close friend, Barbara Preston, who was also an active member of First Church. In the course of the conversation, Barbara alluded to the relationship her twenty-two-year-old daughter, Joan, was having with "that charming Dr. Peter Donovan." As Murray listened to Barbara's delight over her daughter's new love, she realized that the daughter was sexually involved with Pete Donovan. Now she knew why he wanted to keep his sexual relationship with her secret. Murray's ambivalence was resolved: She knew that a sexual relationship with Pete Donovan was not what she needed. She contacted Donovan and broke off the relationship. The next day he came to her house and they talked at length. Murray told him then that although his private life was his business, he should not "fool around" with the young women in the church. He denied any involvement with Joan Preston; he explained that she had pursued him for two years. In fact, he explained, he had a real problem with women pursuing him. Donovan persisted in the face of Murray's very clear attempt to end the relationship. Even that day he suggested they have sex again. She continued to say "no" at every turn, and he did not force her. He continued to call her for a brief period, but Murray refused to respond. This seemed finally to convince him of her unequivocal decision.

Even though her sexual relationship with Pete Donovan had been secret, Murray knew she had entered into it honestly. She now realized that he had not. She felt misused, taken advantage of, and betrayed. She also felt foolish and embarrassed to have been so gullible. Murray never had seen herself as naive before. Now she realized how vulnerability could make a person do strange things.

Murray began to listen with a second ear to stories she was hearing about Pete Donovan's activities. Many things she had previously dismissed she now paid attention to. The more stories Murray heard, the more uncomfortable she became. She worried particularly about younger women, who might not be as resilient as she was and who would be even more vulnerable to Pete Donovan's charms. When she heard about Kristin Stone, she decided that something had to be done. Stone was twenty-one years old when Pete Donovan assaulted her in 1981. Stone's mother told Murray about her daughter's experience in June of that year. It was then that Murray realized that Donovan had been involved with Joan Preston, Kristin Stone, and herself all at the same time. She began to wonder how many more women he had taken advantage of. Kristin Stone's mother pleaded with Murray not to tell anyone else. She said it was all over and done with and no one else need know; she was concerned that any further discussion would damage Stone's reputation. At this point, Murray did not know what to do and did nothing. In retrospect, she wished that she had not waited to act.

In November 1981, Donovan contacted Murray and asked her to dinner. He said that he wanted to discuss a project at First Church and needed her help to raise funds for it. She went to dinner with him and took advantage of the situation to confront him: She told him that she not only knew about Joan Preston, but also about others in the church with whom he was sexually involved. She said that she felt this was totally inappropriate for the minister and was very concerned that this was going on. He simply denied that anything of this kind was occurring and said that he would never do anything harmful to anyone. He agreed that if these things were true, she should be concerned. He said that he would not want a minister who was taking advantage of women in the church. He painted himself as the all-American, true and pure, who would challenge any such behavior in a fellow pastor. He denied any impropriety on his part. Murray retorted that she had no doubt that the information the women had shared with her had been truthful and that she thought he needed help. He simply dismissed her concern, saying it was not a problem. Murray was surprised and troubled by his vehement denial. She knew that she would have to do something more to deal with this problem.

Kristin Stone

In 1960, when she was an infant, Kristin Stone's parents brought her to First Church. She was confirmed there as a young teenager. First Church was the only church home she had ever known and it was a very significant part of her childhood and teenage years. She was a contemporary of Joan Preston. Gifted in dance, Stone had found the church to be a source of encouragement for her as she developed her talent.

In the fall of 1980, at about the same time that the new pastor, Dr. Pete Donovan, officiated at Marian Murray's niece's wedding, he approached Stone and asked her to start a special after-school children's program at First Church. In this capacity, she would become a volunteer member of the church staff. This was an exciting prospect for the twenty-one-year-old college student. She eagerly accepted and immediately began to develop the children's program.

During the next few months, Stone found Donovan approachable and helpful. One Sunday after services, as she spoke to him in the receiving line, he said warmly, "Let me get to know you." She was pleased that he seemed to reach out to her; she thought of him as an older brother or even as a father figure. This was important to her, since her own father had died just one year before. The fact that Donovan was her pastor and older than she meant that she looked up to him and trusted him. She would occasionally go to him to discuss some faith question she was considering. Although she did not seek counseling from him, she enjoyed their conversations immensely.

Stone was sexually inexperienced. Although she had dated boys in high school, she had not been sexually active with them. She noticed that Donovan began to make flirtatious remarks to her, but in her naiveté Stone thought he was teasing her like an older brother might. She was flattered by his attention. He made her feel mature and womanly. As the suggestive comments continued, she began to realize that he was not kidding. She then thought that she must be misinterpreting his intent and dismissed these incidents from her mind, ashamed that she would think such things about her pastor.

Six months later, in mid-March 1981, Stone visited her former dance teacher, whom she dearly loved and who was then terminally ill with cancer. She was far more traumatized by this visit than she had anticipated. She realized that her strong feelings probably related to her grief at the death of her father. All of these feelings came to the fore for Stone, and she went to First Church to seek the counsel of her pastor. Donovan could tell she was upset and gently led her into one of the Sunday school rooms to talk. He put his arms around her and said, "You really do need someone to take care of you, don't you?" Stone was distraught and was grateful for the reassurance and affection she felt from Donovan. He kissed her and then led her into his office and closed the door so they could, he said, talk privately.

She was relieved for the opportunity to talk about her feelings and the difficulty of seeing her dance teacher in such pain. But instead of talking, Donovan continued to kiss Stone. Her initial feeling of comfort and reassurance quickly turned to surpise and fear. He began removing her clothing. She did not know what he was doing or why. She was too stunned even to react. She submitted to sexual intercourse with him on the floor of his office.

Stone had never had sexual intercourse before. This all seemed so unreal. A wave of nausea swept over her. She wanted to cry out; she wanted to run away. But she feared Donovan's disapproval if she challenged him. She feared his anger if she tried to leave. Stone felt she had no option. Her first experience of genital sexual contact was rape. In tears, she dressed and left.

When she returned home, Stone was clearly upset and immediately shared with her mother that something sexual had occurred with Pete Donovan. But she felt awkward and was unable to tell her mother specifically what had happened. Her mother did not pursue the discussion with her. She did not seem to want to know what had gone on, but she assumed from what little Stone had said that she and Pete Donovan were dating and had had an argument. The argument must have been about sex; she said to her daughter, "There is no use crying over spilled milk." She implied that Stone must have been the cause of whatever had happened. Stone did not bring up her assault again with anyone until six months later.

A week after the rape, Pete Donovan visited Stone at her home. She felt conflicted. She was not sure herself what had happened to her. She wanted to see him because she was still emotionally tied to him, but she also felt numb and depressed about their encounter a week earlier. She felt guilty for whatever it was that had happened, yet she was clear that any further sexual contact with Pete Donovan was out of the question. He suggested that they go to the church, where he had work to do, and that they could talk there. Stone felt desperate to talk with someone and so went with Donovan.

When they got to the church, Donovan took Stone into his office and then asked her to hug him. She responded, hoping to keep him from being angry with her. Again he proceeded to disrobe her. This time she knew what he was doing, but even more than before, she felt overwhelmed by him. She submitted again to sexual intercourse. Again she went away feeling dazed, empty, and alone, believing that she could tell no one. Who would believe her? Who could possibly understand?

Stone continued her work at First Church with the children's program. She managed to avoid contact with Donovan as much as possible. She still told no one he had raped her, because she was afraid that no one would believe her.

Three months later, in early June, Stone directed a dance program at the church. Afterward, Donovan asked her to stay and talk with him. She felt anxious and uncomfortable with his request, but he had not approached her since March and she hoped that those past encounters were gone, forgotten, and never to be repeated. Other people were still in the church that night, and she assumed that he would not try anything. Donovan closed the door to his office and told Stone that he thought she might be the one for him to marry. Once again a mixture of feelings washed over her; she was surprised and flattered, isolated and frightened, empty and alone. She did not know what to think. Did Donovan really love her? Was the previous unwanted sexual activity his way of showing his love? How could she not be thrilled at the prospect of marriage to Donovan? Would her minister suggest doing anything that was wrong? Who could she talk this over with? Why didn't Donovan care about what she wanted? Why did he scare her so? Stone submitted to sexual intercourse again.

As the weeks passed without seeing him, Stone's confusion was beginning to gel into anger. She realized that she had been taken advantage of by someone whom she trusted and respected. Donovan came to her house several weeks later and again suggested that she have sex with him. This time she showed him to the door, told him how angry she was at the way he had treated her, and that she would not let him do it again. He responded, "Who's going to believe you? I am the minister. You'll get the worst of this if you tell. I can say you went after me." Stone feared that he was right. Again she told no one.

On July 2, 1981, Donovan stopped by Stone's house and invited her to go to a friend's home to play croquet. She did not want to go with him, but she wanted to talk to him about what had happened and make him see how she felt about it. She felt that it would be safe because they would be in public. After the croquet, Donovan drove Stone to an isolated area and told her to have sex with him. She refused and told him to take her home. She did not want any sexual contact with him and she let him know that unequivocally. This time she had the strength to resist his approach. When they arrived at her home, she asked him to leave; Donovan refused and followed her in. Stone was late for a dance rehearsal and so left Donovan in the living room and went to her room to get ready. When she returned he was still there, and she tried to usher him out the door. Donovan then picked Stone up and carried her into her mother's bedroom. She tried to get away. He pulled her clothing off and tried to sexually penetrate her. Stone was crying and yelling, "No, no" as loud as she could while holding her hands over the opening to her vagina to prevent his penis from entering her. She succeeded at least in this; he ejaculated outside of her body. Then he left her house.

Angry and wanting to prevent any further approaches by Donovan, Stone called him several days later and told him that she never wanted to see him again and that he needed psychiatric help very badly. Donovan screamed obscenities at her over the phone. Still she could tell no one.

In the fall of 1981, Stone went away to college and was very careful to not let anyone at First Church know her address or phone number. She did not want Donovan to be able to find her. She was afraid of him. But somehow he got her phone number and called, saying he wanted to see her. Although she made it clear that she did not want to see him, she was constantly afraid that he would appear and approach her again.

During that year at college, Stone sought therapy from a counselor to help her deal with her anxiety and depression. Finally, she was able to tell someone about her experience with Donovan. Much to her relief, she was believed. In therapy Stone received some affirmation of her perception that she had been used, and she came to realize that she also had been raped. She thought someone else should know what had happened. But her therapist warned her that women in her situation were usually blamed regardless of what they had suffered. Stone decided that she had nothing to gain from telling anyone else, and she convinced herself that hers was probably an isolated case anyway.

It took Stone two more years to come to terms with her experience and to discover that she was not the only one, but was one among many. Her anger rushed to the surface. It cleansed and mobilized her to try to stop Donovan. Finding other women who knew exactly what she was talking about gave her the courage to act.

Katie Simpson

Rev. Katie Simpson was a young pastor in the District. Following her ordination in 1977, she had served a small church from 1977 to 1979. She first became aware of Dr. Pete Donovan in the summer of 1980, when she heard from some of the teenage girls who had attended church camp that Donovan had propositioned them there. He was codirector of the camp that summer, the same summer when he began to date Joan Preston. Simpson's first contact with the First Church of Newburg was also in the summer of 1980, when she directed the vacation church school for the children. In this capacity, she began to get to know the members of First Church, but she had very little contact with Pete Donovan. Simpson's first extended meeting with Donovan came in February 1981, at a meeting for future camp directors. At this meeting, Simpson observed what she recalls as "interesting" dynamics between Donovan and another woman in the meeting. As she watched these interchanges, she realized how uneasy she felt being around Donovan.

In the spring of 1981, she was hired as a consultant at First Church by the director of Christian education. It was during this period that Donovan was still dating Joan Preston and assaulting Kristin Stone. Soon after Simpson went to work there, Donovan met with her and told her how pleased he was that she was assisting the director of Christian education. He invited her to lunch, saying that he was interested in her becoming the associate minister of First Church. Due to other commitments, Simpson was not interested in the job offer at that time, but agreed to discuss it. They set a date for lunch.

For reasons she did not realize until later, Simpson felt uneasy even then, and so decided to take her two young daughters along for the lunch meeting. At some point during the lunch, conversation shifted to Simpson's current family situation. She mentioned that her husband was then working out of state and that she and he were struggling with some very serious issues in their marriage. As the conversation progressed, Simpson realized that Donovan's demeanor toward her shifted. He began to approach her more like a suitor than a colleague. She grew even more uncomfortable and more thankful that she had brought her daughters along.

When lunch concluded and Simpson prepared to get into her car, Donovan reached for her and gave her a messy kiss on the mouth; then he laughed and said, "I've never seen a face so shocked!" Simpson replied in anger, "My colleagues don't usually kiss me like that!" She drove home with her daughters and tried to put the incident out of her mind.

Soon afterward, Donovan called Simpson and asked to see her again. He referred somewhat obliquely to "not being able to control himself." Simson naively disregarded his comment and discouraged his initiation of a social relationship. She continued her work at First Church.

Donovan called Simpson again at home, supposedly for business purposes. In the middle of the conversation about church matters, he said, "I jack off every night just thinking about you." Simpson was so astonished by such an inappropriate and tasteless comment that she decided she must have misunderstood him and ignored it. Months later Simpson marveled at her denial.

Another call from Donovan several days later brought another sexual proposition. This time his meaning was clear: He said that he wanted to have sex with her. Simpson was shocked and bewildered by his presumption of sexual access. In tears, she defended herself against his advances by saying, "Pete, don't you realize I'm married?" Simpson finally realized that her assumption that she and Donovan shared a professional, collegial relationship was inaccurate. She expected to be treated as a professional peer, not as a readily available sex object. She quit her job at First Church.

During this time, Simpson was also a part-time chaplain at a hospital. In this capacity, she made a number of presentations to local churches and groups about the chaplaincy program. On one such occasion, not long after leaving First Church, she was preparing to speak to the Newburg Ministerial Association. Donovan, who seldom attended the Ministerial Association meetings, appeared and approached Simpson as she was setting up her materials. He asked if she would sleep with him at the upcoming denominational annual meeting. Simpson replied with an insistent "No," but Donovan continued to press her until she began her presentation. She left immediately afterward, avoiding further contact with him.

Following this incident, she contacted Rev. Ralph Bennett, associate District minister of her denomination, and told him of Donovan's approach. Bennett was concerned that Donovan should be behaving so unprofessionally and was supportive of Simpson's reproach of Donovan. Believing this to be sufficient, he took no action at this point.

Simpson's strategy of carefully avoiding Donovan seemed effective. The exception was occasional courtesy greetings at denominational meetings, where all seemed quite normal and professional, as if none of the preceding encounters had occurred. Simpson regained some of her sense of confidence and safety in Donovan's presence at public gatherings.

She next crossed Donovan's path in the fall. A member of First Church invited Simpson to speak to the senior citizens' group. Simpson hesitated, but then felt that sufficient time had passed since her unpleasant experiences with First Church and decided to accept the invitation. After her lecture, the church secretary asked her to stop by Donovan's study before she left. Again she hesitated, and assessed the situation: There were a lot of people around in the church, so she decided that the near presence of others would provide some measure of safety for her. She entered his study.

Unexpectedly, Donovan closed the door. He then turned to her without a word, picked her up, dropped her on his sofa, and got on top of her. He casually mentioned that he was glad she had worn a dress, but cursed that she had on panty hose, which he pulled down to her knees. He then forced his finger into her vagina. He said, "Now, doesn't that feel good? Just pretend you are Mrs. Donovan." Simpson now understood all she had heard about rape victims being too frightened to scream. She was stunned and terrified. She could feel that he was heavy and strong as he held her down. She opened her mouth, but no sound came out. As he leaned back to unzip his pants, she struggled against him. When he leaned forward she jabbed her elbow to his throat and rolled out from under him. She then ran out of his study to her car; she drove herself home and tried not to think about what had just happened to her.

Later that day, Simpson said to her husband, "The pastor at Newburg jumped me in his office today." Then she burst into tears. Her husband responded, "These male ministers—I don't know why they don't leave you alone." With that the conversation ended. Simpson successfully blocked the trauma of her experience for several months. She vowed never to go to First Church again and never to have any occasion to encounter Pete Donovan again. She told herself that it was not really rape, since he had not penetrated her with his penis. Still, she was ashamed. She blamed herself; if she had not gone there, this would never have happened. She feared that no one would even believe this had happened. She could not think of a single colleague in whom she could confide. She felt alone, angry, and hurt. These things happen to other people, not to her. Up until then, she had felt invincible.

She told no one else until November, four months after the assault. Again, in conversation with Ralph Bennett, she used the euphemism, saying that Donovan had "jumped" her in his office. She could not bring herself to say exactly what had happened. Bennett was still concerned; but, based on what she was saying, did not feel that there was sufficient evidence of misconduct to necessitate District action.

Then Simpson began to worry about the other women. She knew enough to know that these incidents are seldom isolated. As a pastor, she worried that other women pastors might be in danger of being harmed by Pete Donovan. She also worried about the women parishioners at First Church.

She told other women clergy in the area about her experience. Anytime she heard Donovan's name come up in conversation, she would tell them what he had done to her. She was warning them that he was dangerous and that they should be careful around him: Any woman was fair game. None of her female colleagues seemed surprised to learn of her experience; they had heard about Pete Donovan before.

Bernie Mitchell

Bernie Mitchell had been a member of First Church for fifty-five years and served diligently on many committees and boards. Although she had not been active during the years immediately prior to Dr. Pete Donovan's coming to First Church, she was attracted to his style and approach to the ministry. She became active again. He seemed warm, friendly, and inspiring. But Mitchell remembers that even in the beginning of Donovan's ministry at

First Church, his unusually personalized and intense approach to individuals was disquieting to her.

Mitchell's first personal contact with Donovan took place at the First Church Christmas party in 1981. He took her aside from the party and told her of his plans to develop a special outreach ministry through one of the local tourist attractions near Newburg. She initially felt that the plans were somewhat grandiose, but she was intrigued with the possibility of reaching a large number of people. Donovan asked her to help him implement this plan. Mitchell agreed and became heavily involved in the effort.

Early in 1982, Donovan again approached Mitchell with an idea: He wanted her to fill the vacant position of director of singles ministry at First Church. In offering this volunteer position to her, he indicated that it was quite an honor to be asked to serve on his staff, and he made it clear that he expected her loyalty to him in all church matters. Mitchell *was* honored; she was delighted at the prospect of working for Donovan. His charisma had charmed her; she expected that it would be a delight to work with him so closely.

A few months later, Donovan made still another offer to Mitchell. He wanted her also to take on responsibility for special programs for First Church. Donovan told her that she was the only person he would even consider for this important task. This suggestion of an expanded staff role thrilled Mitchell. She knew that this meant that Donovan was pleased with her and her work.

This affirmation from her pastor meant a lot to Mitchell at this time in her life. She was sixty years old. Ten years earlier, she had had a mastectomy and had struggled with the subsequent loss of self-worth. During this period, she was also divorced, which further undermined her sense of self and place in the world. Pete Donovan's praise began to restore her self-confidence; his reliance on her as one of his key staff reassured her of her competence and worthiness.

Donovan's attention to Bernie Mitchell, however, did not stop with verbal stroking. It became commonplace that after every private conversation with him in his office, they would end up in a sexual embrace. He would hold Mitchell, kiss and hug her. This attention progressed to rubbing his genitals against her and running his hands under her blouse. These encounters took place on the average of once a week.

Since her mastectomy, Mitchell had not felt comfortable with any intimate touching by a man. When Donovan began to be affectionate with her, she was pleased and enjoyed the reassurance of his touch. When the affection became sexual, she continued to find it pleasurable. He never forced his attentions on her. He never suggested further sexual involvement or sexual intercourse. She was seduced by his charm and did not initially question the appropriateness of his attention to her. She felt special and privileged to be so close to him.

During this same period of time that she was serving on his staff, a strange series of events occurred. Mitchell began to receive phone calls from Donovan in the middle of the night. Although the calls usually started out light and friendly, they invariably ended up with Donovan ranting and raving about church memberes. He named the "fucking people at church who were out to get him" or pointed out the "stupidity" of the people at church: "It's my church and no Goddamed fucking bastard is going to tell me what to do!"

Sometimes his verbal abuse would turn on Mitchell: He would call her names and threaten to fire her. She began to regard these experiences as "verbal pistol whippings." Sometimes she would hang up on him and he would call back, continuing to threaten her. Always the next morning he would call and apologize profusely. Although these middle-of-the-night calls upset Mitchell, she would always accept his apology and explain away his bizarre behavior by telling herself that he was under a lot of stress, that people at First Church did not understand him, and so forth. She remained enamored of him and did not question his actions. To her he was a sincere, loving, and very talented pastor who cared deeply for her.

Bernie Mitchell only began to doubt this picture of Pete Donovan when she started to hear the rumors about Donovan's involvement with other women. He had told her that she was the only one in the church whom he could trust, and he would confide things in her that he had "never told another living human being." As she compared notes with several other women, Mitchell realized that they had been told the exact same things. He had promised her a promotion on the church staff; he had promised the same promotion to other staff members. As the pieces fell into place, Mitchell began to realize that she had been used and betrayed by Donovan. Mitchell felt stupid for having let herself be duped. She resigned from her staff position at First Church just before Easter 1984.

Mitchell confronted Donovan about his sexual involvement with other women in the church. He acknowledged that he had been involved with some women from the church and went on to explain why. He said that when he first came to First Church, his fiancée was visiting from out of town. When he went to the motel to pick her up, he found a note from her saying that she could not go through with the marriage. He said, "I went crazy and went out and screwed every woman I could get my hands on during the next several weeks." This rejection by his fiancée was somehow supposed to justify his behavior. But he implied that since then, there had been no other sexual activity with women from the church. Mitchell was not so easily convinced.

A friend told her about Marian Murray. Murray shared her story with Mitchell and told her that several women were considering a formal complaint to the District. Mitchell decided to join them. Even though her sexual contact with Donovan had not included intercourse as theirs had, the betrayal she felt was no less intense. She was angry about his obvious deception of her and others, and she could see the effect it was having on First Church. She wanted someone to stop Donovan.

Nancy Linder

Nancy Linder joined First Church in 1978, and so was a relatively new member when Donovan became pastor. She attended worship services regularly and served as a deaconess for one year.

Her husband helped in the Sunday school. But Linder was not widely known in the congregation.

Early in 1983, when she and her husband began having problems in their marriage, Linder went to her pastor without hesitation. She thought that Dr. Peter Donovan would be able to counsel her. She saw him individually for counseling occasionally during the next year; she and her husband also went to see him several times together.

When Linder called and asked to see Donovan in February 1984, he was available and she went right over to the church. She said she was having difficulty in her marriage: She said that her husband was abusing her verbally and physically, and she was growing increasingly afraid of him. In the course of this counseling session, Donovan told Linder that her husband was very lucky to have such a lovely, sensuous wife. Linder was flattered; she had been hearing the opposite from her husband for so long that hearing this compliment from her pastor made her feel lovable again. But she was aware of mixed messages from Donovan; she was getting a strong sexual come-on from him. She dealt with it by stating clearly that she was not looking for an affair; she had enough problems to deal with right now.

When the counseling session concluded and she got up to leave the office, Linder casually said that she just wished she could get some magic back into her marriage. Donovan responded by saying that she was magic, and then he put his arms around her and began stroking her hair. He said that he had been in love with her for two years and that she was wonderful and desirable. In one sense, this was just what Linder thought she needed to hear from a man. What she termed her husband's abuse had all but destroyed her sense of herself as an attractive, lovable woman. She was easily taken in by Donovan's attentions. He asked if he could come over to her house so that their conversation could be more informal. Eager to spend more time with him, she agreed. He followed her home, but there was no conversation, formal or informal. There Donovan had sexual intercouse with her while her husband was at work. Taken in by his flattering advances,

Linder willingly agreed to this sexual activity, which was repeated on three other occasions. This attention from an attractive, charming man whom she had known and trusted as her pastor seemed wonderful at the time.

Yet Linder was also uncomfortable. She realized that she was not getting what she was looking for. Whenever she would ask for Donovan's advice in handling the abuse, he simply said that he could not deal with that. Whenever she was with Donovan, she was still seeking counsel about her marriage; his response was, "When we are together, let's not talk about your problems."

Linder had also sought advice from Donovan about infertility. Linder had been artificially inseminated, but had not conceived. She was considering the idea of approaching a friend to be a donor, an arrangement which would be made through a lawyer. Since this was a somewhat unorthodox approach, she decided to discuss it with her pastor, Peter Donovan. He supported the plan and encouraged her to proceed. Later when Linder went to see Donovan for counseling, he offered to be the donor she was seeking: He offered to impregnate her. This was not the counsel she was expecting from her pastor.

Linder then heard some upsetting news: A friend told her that Donovan was a violent man and a womanizer, and cautioned her that she should not be in counseling with him. Linder was disturbed and frightened, but still disbelieving. Her friend gave her the name of a woman who had been involved with Donovan: Marian Murray. Linder contacted Murray and heard a story very similar to her own. She was convinced; the more she thought about it, the more unnerved and fearful she became. Here she was going to Donovan for counseling because of the violence and abuse she was experiencing at home, only to learn that the person who was counseling her was also abusive. She avoided Donovan and did not return for counseling.

At the end of April, Donovan called Linder at work and asked why she had not called him. She said that she was very concerned about her marriage and really wanted to work on the problems with her husband. Donovan's reply was, "So what?" He then quizzed her: Had anyone said anything to her? Assuming that he was referring to his sexual involvement with other women at First Church, she avoided his question and said "No." By then she was afraid of what he might do if he knew how much she knew. Linder was frightened of Donovan, afraid to see him and afraid to tell him she would not see him. Her strategy was to avoid him. He finally stopped calling her.

Belatedly, Linder realized that Donovan had no real interest in her marriage or in her well-being. She acknowledged her mistake of agreeing to a sexual relationship with Donovan when her real concern had been her marriage. She also recognized his manipulation of her. He had sworn her to secrecy about their sexual relationship. She now knew that he had sworn other women to secrecy as well; she no longer felt bound by her promise. Linder was the most current of Donovan's victims, and she was ready to do whatever she could to stop him. When she became aware that other women were discussing what Donovan had done to them, she was eager to join. When she met the women, Joan Preston was the only one she knew; they had served together as deaconesses at First Church. She was relieved to meet the others and ready to act.

A Familiar Pattern

As I listened to the women's stories, I began to see a familiar pattern that echoed stories I had heard from other victims. I was not surprised that any of them had fallen prey to their pastor. The circumstances of their lives made them susceptible to an offender like Pete Donovan. And yet the circumstances of their lives are not that different from those of most women. They and others were the unlucky ones who happened to cross Donovan's path.

Their stories illustrated the primary dimensions of ethical violation that result from pastoral misconduct: exploitation of vulnerability, misuse of authority, absence of authentic consent, and creation of dual relationships. In addition, there were the instances of sexual assault, a gross violation of ethics in any relationship.

For Peter Donovan to initiate a sexual relationship with Marian Murray while she was still grieving her husband's death and was seeking help for her child was a calculating play on her vulnerability. To be vulnerable is to be without defense and thus open to harm. Consequently, one can be readily seduced and manipulated by a person who is perceived as trustworthy and powerful. Because of the circumstances of her life at this time, this ordinarily assertive, self-directed, confident woman was a relatively easy target for Donovan's controlling charm. This involvement with Donovan clearly was not in *her* best interest. It resulted in depriving her of the pastoral relationship she needed and had sought in order to deal with her son's problems, and presented her with an additional issue in her own life.

Marian Murray believed that she had consented to Pete Donovan's initiation of sex. She engaged in the sexual activity freely. He did not force her. But in fact she did not freely choose because she did not have that opportunity. Consent to sexual activity, in order to be authentic, must take place in a context of mutuality, choice, full knowledge, and equal power, and in the absence of coercion or fear. When there is an imbalance of power in a relationship, these necessary factors will not be present. Both Donovan and Murray chose to be sexually active with each other and saw themselves as "consenting adults"; but because he was her pastor and she a parishioner seeking counsel, they were not peers and the "consent" was not authentic. The consequence to Murray of this inauthentic consent was not clear at first; but as the sexual relationship progressed, she became more confused, her expectations began to conflict, and she began to feel Donovan's coercion. Murray, the person with less power in the relationship, began to realize that her freedom to choose and shape the relationship was limited; Donovan was manipulating and controlling her. Authentic consent, which is necessary for a just and emotionally satisfying sexual relationship, was absent. When Murray realized what had happened to her as she saw the wider context of Donovan's sexual conduct, she was able to break off her relationship with him and confront him. Some others were not so successful as she.

Pete Donovan misused his authority as a pastor in his relationship with Kristin Stone. She knew little about relationships and less about sex. At first she trusted his judgment and his concern for her well-being, because he was her pastor. He was able to see her when he pleased because she was a volunteer employee and a young, unsophisticated parishioner. His pastoral authority and charm easily overcame the sensible hesitations Kristin Stone was feeling. With her there was no illusion of consent. Donovan consistently used verbal and physical coercion to force her to have sexual intercourse. She was a victim of acquaintance rape by her pastor.

Pete Donovan dated and courted Joan Preston in an attempt to establish and maintain a dual relationship, to engage in both a personal and professional relationship with her at the same time. In public he was her pastor, but in private he was her lover. He used the veil of secrecy to insure that this distinction was clearly maintained. The relationship shifted from that of pastor/parishioner to lover/lover, except that he never acknowledged this shift or its implications. Donovan used his pastoral role as a source of credibility with Preston so that when he proposed marriage, she trusted his sincerity. Yet now she had no pastor to whom to turn for counsel about this new relationship and possible marriage. Pete Donovan had deprived her of that resource.

A pastor who is called to serve a congregation fulfills a particular role for the individuals in the congregation. Expectations, stated and unstated, are established. The parishioners expect that the person in the role of pastor brings gifts, skills, and resources which they can call upon as needed. The members of First Church clearly recognized the gifts Pete Donovan brought to them from the very beginning. Their response was admiration and respect for his skill as a pastor. But he was, formally and informally, their *pastor*: This professional role should have defined his relationship to the membership.

Unlike the professions of medicine or law, ministry is liable to a blurring of roles: Friendships do develop with parishioners with whom one spends a great deal of professional *and* social time.

Particularly for the pastor who is single, the temptation to confuse roles may be great. On the one hand, a personal relationship is private (although lived out in the public arena) and is the means by which one legitimately seeks to meet one's own primary emotional, spiritual, and sexual needs. In contrast, a professional relationship is public (although often experienced in private), rests within a context of external standards of responsibility, and carries the expectation that the professional act in the best interests of those whom he or she serves.[1]

Just as the doctor, therapist, and lawyer do not practice their professions on their family members, neither should clergy presume to be able to carry out dual relationships. A minister cannot responsibly be pastor/counselor *and* lover/partner with the same person at the same time. This dual relationship will result in conflicts of expectations and interest in which it is likely that the pastor's self-interest will take priority over the interests of the parishioner. The parishioner will then be deprived of a safe place to seek counsel and support for her or his own agenda. It is unwise, impractical, and unethical for a pastor to engage in dual relationships. It is, in fact, impossible. Pete Donovan seldom allowed his role as professional minister to limit his relationships with parishioners. Consequently, he attempted to engage in many dual relationships.

Rev. Katie Simpson was a colleague of Dr. Pete Donovan, or so she thought, and eventually a member of his staff. As such, she initially had no hesitation about being around him. She presumed, until she learned otherwise, that he would treat her with the respect and the professional courtesy she deserved. She was an attractive, bright, self-assured clergywoman. For Donovan, she was a real challenge. He carefully cultivated Simpson's vulnerabilities. Donovan no doubt knew that employment and job security for clergywomen are hard to come by. In offering Simpson a position as his associate, he believed he was making her an offer she could not refuse, an opportunity to join his inner circle, a paid staff position. Simpson was certainly troubled about her marriage difficulties, and she inadvertently shared this with Donovan. He presumed to have a green light to pursue her. When she refused Donovan, she raised the stakes even higher in his eyes. Again, the question of consent would never enter this picture. Donovan used physical force to penetrate Simpson vaginally with his finger. This too is rape.

Bernie Mitchell's vulnerability was multi-layered. Her age and the most recent circumstances of her life, including her divorce and bout with cancer, meant that she was emotionally susceptible to the attentions of a caring man. The fact that the man who gave her attention was her pastor meant that she never questioned his intentions. She was also a volunteer staff member of First Church and Peter Donovan was her boss. In this role, he had the power to give or take away her job, which had become very important to her. Because Mitchell was convinced that Donovan was exceptionally gifted as a pastor, she minimized and excused his irrational behavior even though it was terribly upsetting to her. She accepted the role of suffering servant to him because she was taken in by his brilliant, though mercurial, personality. She was duped by Donovan, who convinced her that she held a special place in his life. Only when she realized that she was one among many did she begin to pay attention to her better judgment.

Nancy Linder was a battered woman who went to her pastor for help. Her self-image and confidence had been badly shaken by abuse. She was looking for something to change all this: pregnancy, couples' counseling. She needed information and support from her pastor. She went to Pete Donovan because she believed he could provide what she needed. When Donovan initiated sexual activity with Nancy Linder under these circumstances, he misused the authority of the pastoral role to override her hesitation. Donovan easily seduced Nancy Linder because she thought he represented everything that her husband was not: a caring, gentle, attentive man who thought she was wonderful. She became a willing participant, but she was not consenting. She was in no position to consent authentically.

Even if Nancy Linder had initiated the sexual relationship with Donovan, he would still have been responsible. It is certainly not unusual for a parishioner to be attracted to her minister. Ministers frequently appear to embody those attractive qualities that may be missing in a person's relational life. The parishioner may in fact be attracted to the power of the role itself. But the pastor who responds affirmatively to a sexual initiative by a parishioner allows the boundaries of the pastoral relationship to be broken. The pastor has the power and the responsibility to maintain these boundaries in order to preserve the pastoral relationship.[2] This serves the best interest of the parishioner *and* the best interests of the pastor.

The pastoral role by its very nature gives the pastor access to people's lives on a very immediate and intimate level. The occasions of the most intense contact with a pastor are frequently occasions of life crisis or passage such as illness, death, marriage, or divorce. The pastor is the only helping professional who can initiate contact with a client. A minister can walk into a parishioner's home uninvited in order to fulfill pastoral duties. This access and the authority the pastor brings to the relationship can be invaluable to a parishioner in a personal or family crisis. But it is also an opportunity for an unethical pastor to misuse this power and authority. Peter Donovan exploited this opportunity.

Another Woman: Lina Robinson

Not all of the women at First Church were as vulnerable to Peter Donovan as the women who initially came together to deal with the problem he had created. Although Lina Robinson was not a firsthand victim, she believed what she heard about Pete Donovan: It was consistent with what she saw of him.

She had been a member of First Church for thirty-six years and had served on nearly all of the boards and committees in the congregation. She was, without question, a pillar. In 1979, she was serving as a deaconess and on the search committee looking for a new pastor. Her first impression as she perused Peter Donovan's résumé during the search process was guardedly optimistic—she was the one who thought that he was too good to be true. The committee concurred and jokingly commented that he should be able to walk on water. One committee member suggested that he looked like a shooting star. But Robinson and the others were singularly impressed by his paper credentials and by his personal presence. She voted to call Peter Donovan to be the pastor of First Church.

In 1980, she was serving as moderator of the District, but she was still heavily involved in the work of First Church. When she first heard about the information alleging misconduct by Pete Donovan, she believed it to be true. She had been concerned earlier about the amount of counseling Donovan was doing. It seemed to her that he was counseling too many people, and for long stretches of time. Even then she felt that this was not the task for which he had been hired at First Church, and she discussed her concern with him. His response to her was that he did things differently than this church was used to, but that he would be careful.

Robinson had also encouraged Donovan to work with the District on a number of local church concerns, in order to seek assistance or financial resources for special projects as well as to share ideas and new initiatives. As moderator of the District, she knew well that the District would be interested and supportive and was herself invested in maintaining this working relationship between First Church and the denomination. Donovan opposed her suggestions at every turn. He did not want the District meddling in First Church affairs or blocking new program ideas. It was clear to her that Donovan wanted to keep as much distance as possible between himself and the District structure. Donovan began to see Robinson as a "denomination person," which meant that he could not control her. He tried to steer clear of her whenever possible.

In the fall of 1981, about a year and a half into Donovan's pastorate at First Church, a young woman came to see Robinson. She was an old family friend whom Robinson had taught in Sunday school. The young woman was very upset and wanted to talk to Robinson. She thought she knew what it was about and said to the young woman, "Don't tell me anything you don't want to." Robinson suspected that the woman was sexually involved with Donovan, but she did not want to hear about it from her then. Fearful and unprepared, Robinson did not think that she could do anything with that piece of information. She could tell that the young woman was distraught, and Robinson told her that although she doubted that she could help her, she should talk to someone who could. But Robinson did not want to get involved.

During this period, Donovan had begun to talk with the deacons about how he was being maligned by stories that were beginning to circulate in the congregation. He would never discuss any of this with the deaconesses. Robinson was not pleased with this situation, and she went to one of the deacons and questioned why the women were left out of these discussions. Other deaconesses were disturbed by this as well. At this point it seemed mostly to be a puzzle to them, and yet they clearly began to feel shunted aside.

Some of the deaconesses had other concerns, which they brought to each other. They began to hear of situations where Donovan had broken furniture in the church and thrown things around. They were confused: What should they do about this? How should they deal with this behavior from their pastor? Robinson had experienced Donovan's rage firsthand not long after he came to First Church. He had taken her aside one day and lectured her about one of the other parishioners, whom he never wanted to see hold an office in the church again. Even then she felt his behavior was out of line and it was frightening to her.

In retrospect, Robinson was surprised and disappointed that something like the chaos Pete Donovan created could happen in her church. She trusted her denomination to protect the local church from someone like Donovan. When she read recommendations from the national church office in support of him, she believed them. She felt betrayed by the system. What finally amazed Robinson the most was that Donovan never acknowledged responsibility or any sense of wrongdoing: "Pete thought he had done nothing wrong. To him, every action he has taken has been above and beyond the call of duty. He believes that he is right."

Although Lina Robinson was not a primary victim of Pete Donovan, she was a secondary victim, as were all the members of First Church. Because she was not readily vulnerable to him, he avoided her. Robinson was astute enough to realize that there was a serious problem brewing in her church, but, bereft of the means to address it, she closed her ears to explicit information about Donovan's conduct and waited. But once the house of cards began to fall, she was willing to acknowledge that something she never imagined happening in any church had happened in her own.

4. The Church's Response: "Healing the Wound Lightly"

". . . and from prophet to priest, every one deals falsely. They have healed the wound of my people lightly, saying, 'Peace, peace,' when there is no peace."
JEREMIAH 6:13–14

The situation faced by the First Church of Newburg is an example of what happens when a member of the clergy violates professional ethics. During his four-year tenure, the pastor of First Church misused his pastoral role to approach sexually a number of women in this church. Only six chose to come forward and make formal complaints; others hesitated out of fear or out of loyalty to Peter Donovan. The sexual contact that took place between Donovan and the women ranged from verbal suggestion and seduction to sexual intercourse; on occasion, Donovan used coercion and force. Often he pretended that the sexual activity was part of a relationship, and he always required that it be kept secret.

Donovan's violation was not that he initiated sexual activity per se. Ministers have the same rights as everyone else to seek out an intimate relationship. His violation was that he initiated sexual activity within a pastoral relationship and that he used coercion and deception. Donovan had various pastoral relationships with the women he victimized: Several women had come to Donovan explicitly for counsel; one had sought support as she dealt with her husband's death and her son's resulting crisis; one was an active church volunteer whom he supervised. In addition to these pastoral relationships, one of his victims was a clergywoman who had assumed she had only a collegial relationship with him. Each of these women trusted Donovan not to harm them and to provide for their pastoral needs because he was a minister. They assumed, wrongly in this case, that this meant they were safe with him.

Peter Donovan is a sex offender.[1] He is not the stereotypical sex offender, the sleazy stranger who picks up hitchhikers and rapes them at knife point. He is rather the much more common nice-guy-next-door. At the time of these events, Donovan was also a minister and had been for a number of years. He was widely known and admired by colleagues and parishioners alike. He was trusted and respected. These tools made it possible for him to manipulate and coerce numerous women to whom he had access simply because he was a pastor. His offending pattern ranged from romantic seduction with an erroneous promise of marriage to forcible rape. He seemed to thrive on the power he held over many of the women in his congregation. For many months he succeeded in not being detected by employing the strategy frequently used by incest offenders. He played on the loyalty and ambivalence of his victims and extracted their promise of keeping "our special secret."

The pastoral sex offender does not differ significantly from the secular sex offender. He is manipulative, coercive, controlling, predatory, and sometimes violent. He may also be charming, bright, competent, and charismatic. He is attracted to powerlessness and vulnerability. He is not psychotic, but is usually sociopathic; that is, he has little or no sense of conscience about his offending behaviors. He usually will minimize, lie, and deny when confronted. For these offenders, the ministry presents an ideal opportunity for access to possible victims of all ages.

The only common characteristics of the women who were victimized by Peter Donovan are their female gender and their vulnerability. Otherwise, they are as diverse as the population of church members in general. Their vulnerability was a function of many factors, including age, gender, relationship to Donovan, and their situations of need. Donovan was attracted to these vulnerabilities and exploited them with great skill. Because of his proficiency, it took this church three years to stop him.

The potential of an institution to respond to an internal crisis is determined by its readiness and willingness to face the situation. In the case of the crisis Pete Donovan was creating, neither First

Church nor its District office were ready or willing to hear the revelations the six women brought to them.

Too Little, Too Late

Marian Murray was the first member of First Church to confront Dr. Pete Donovan's unethical conduct in the late fall of 1981. Aware of Donovan's womanizing, and having ended her sexual relationship with him, she told him his behavior was inappropriate for a pastor with parishioners. She told him she knew about other women with whom he was involved. He denied it all and minimized the implications which she believed were clear. He didn't acknowledge what he had done or the harm he had caused. Murray knew her conversation with him had been a waste of time. She realized she would have to go to the leadership of First Church.

In January 1982, one year after her sexual liaison with Donovan, Murray heard of a recent incident in which Donovan had threatened a church member with a baseball bat. This was the final straw for her. She contacted Dan Lawson, the president of the congregation at First Church. Accompanied by Joan Preston, her mother Barbara Preston, and Terry Sarbo (another longtime First Church member and the church school superintendent), Murray met with Lawson. Since Joan Preston had been one of Donovan's first victims, both she and Barbara realized the implications of his misconduct; their concern was to protect First Church from further harm. Sarbo had heard about Donovan's repeated rapes of Kristin Stone and was irate. He had watched Stone growing up in First Church and knew her to be a gifted young woman; he was like an uncle to her. His own experience of Donovan also gave him cause for concern. He had been present at a committee meeting when Donovan, in a rage, put his fist through a wall.

Bolstered by each other, the four talked with the president of First Church. Preston told of her extended dating relationship with Donovan (which she had expected to end in marriage), of the secrecy, the late-night harangues, and the deception. Murray said that she had had "a brief relationship" with Donovan. At this point, she was too embarrassed to go into explicit detail about the sexual nature of that relationship. They told about Kristin Stone. They gave Lawson the names of other families who were willing to tell him of their experiences.

In Dan Lawson, they found a willing ear and felt a genuine response of concern from him. This was not the first time Lawson had heard about Donovan's sexual escapades, but six months earlier it had only been rumors; now he was hearing firsthand. He did not question the sincerity of their reports. These were respected friends and leaders in First Church, and the number of allegations was significant. He assured them that he would deal with the problem. They believed it would be handled internally and quietly with a minimum of commotion and that, as a result, Donovan would leave First Church in the near future. They left the meeting feeling satisfied and relieved. They had told the powers-that-be and they had faith that now the system would respond with dispatch. For them, it was resolved and finished. Marian Murray slept soundly for the first time in over a year.

Several weeks later, Dan Lawson approached Marian Murray at coffee hour after church. He simply said to her, "Did you have intercourse with Donovan?" Murray, although quite taken aback by this abrupt question over tea and cookies said, "Yes." Lawson did not ask any further questions about circumstance or how she felt about the situation. Murray assumed that he was gathering further information in his investigation and she expected some action in the near future.

But nothing happened. Later in the spring, Murray was having lunch with a friend from another congregation. The friend casually mentioned something about Donovan's reputation in the community as a womanizer. Murray was embarrassed and worried that this impression was now being passed around Newburg. She again went to Dan Lawson. She reiterated the need for First Church to deal with this problem. Lawson again agreed that it was a serious matter and that he was worried that people in Newburg were beginning to talk. At this point, she told Lawson she could no longer be a part of a church that did not take ministerial misconduct seriously. She hoped her decision to withdraw from the congregation would impress Lawson with the gravity of this situation.

Seven months after their first converstion with Lawson, in late August 1982, Marian Murray, Terry Sarbo, and Barbara and Joan Preston each received the following letter from him:

Suggestions that there have been pastoral indiscretions have led me to several months of investigation, and many hours of consideration of the courses of action available to me.

I believe that mistakes have been made, but that it is also apparent that there are many evidences of excellent leadership during that time. It may be that the mistakes, which, of course, cannot be corrected, are now behind us, and will not be repeated in the future. It must be said that some of the reports of indiscretions were not supported, or were based upon inaccurate information. Any further reports of unprofessional conduct should give the person involved the opportunity to meet with the dissatisfied party, before some kind of forum, with opportunity to respond to the charges. I believe that such a confrontation at this time would not result in any agreement, and would only be a traumatic experience for all involved. There is no question in my mind that the Church would be severely damaged.

It is my opinion that we should take steps to prevent any future indiscretions, but that we should also recognize and encourage the positive leadership for the betterment of the Church program. Professional counseling will be secured to identify and correct any faults which would tarnish such leadership.

I fully realize that this is not a perfect solution—it is simply the best choice among the alternatives available to me, in my opinion. I will be willing to discuss the matter more fully with anyone who desires to do so.

Murray, Sarbo, and the Prestons were all somewhat dismayed and puzzled by this response. A number of questions remained. What had been the extent of the "investigation"? Marian Murray was certain that Lawson had discussed their complaints with Donovan. But she also believed that Lawson's "investigation" had been limited to that: He had not talked with at least two other church families, whom Murray had suggested were prepared to share their experiences with him. In reference to Donovan,

Lawson acknowledged "mistakes," but he glossed over the serious charges of misconduct. He assured them that "professional counseling" would take care of any problems. He gave no indication that this "professional counseling" would be prepared to address the specifics of Pete Donovan's unethical behavior, nor that this process would be monitored. Lawson suggested that any further reports would require a hearing, which presumably meant involving the leadership of First Church. Yet there was no evidence that Lawson had discussed this problem with any other lay leaders. Lawson did not feel that an open hearing was wise at this time, because it would be traumatic and damaging for the First Church. Did he not see that what Donovan was doing was traumatic and damaging for First Church? Although Lawson acknowledged Donovan's "mistakes," he suggested that this was water under the bridge and that because Donovan had provided excellent leadership, First Church should disregard the charges that were being made and move ahead. Lawson agreed that "we should take steps to prevent any future indiscretions," yet what steps were in fact taken to stop Donovan?

Lawson's carefully worded letter never mentioned Donovan by name and never acknowledged the severity of the complaints. The vagueness of the letter, coupled with an assertion of an investigation which the group knew had not occurred, began to erode their confidence in Lawson's ability to act decisively in this matter. They began to wonder if anything was being done. Instead it felt as if a stone wall was being built, a wall that would protect Donovan and not First Church. Lawson's attempt to reassure Murray, Sarbo, and the Prestons that he had taken care of everything had backfired.

As far as Lawson was concerned, he had dealt with the problem presented by Donovan. He had confronted Donovan about the rumors six months earlier and now about the complaints, and he expected Donovan to shape up. When confronted with the rumors, Donovan had acknowledged his "misbehavior" and promised to be "a good boy." When confronted about the complaints, Donovan denied everything. Lawson was not satisfied with Donovan's responses, but he was reassured to learn that Donovan was in therapy and accepted Donovan's assertion that this would correct his problem. Given the information Marian Murray and Joan Preston were willing to give Lawson, he felt this was all he could do. He chose not to pursue it further with them or others, not to press for more specifics. He also chose not to involve the board of deacons from First Church, a decision he would later regret. At this point, the deacons were mostly Donovan's supporters. Presenting them with the information he had might have headed off Donovan's efforts to procure their unquestioning support during the next few months. In any case, it would have involved the wider leadership in an official process from the beginning and would have prevented Lawson from being isolated in his efforts.

Soon after she received Lawson's letter, Marian Murray attended a meeting with some people from a neighboring church of the same denomination. In the course of the meeting, someone asked her about the situation at First Church. Murray was so frustrated that she poured out some of what had gone on and the difficulty they were having getting any action from the First Church leadership. One member of the group suggested that Murray speak with John Conner, who was then a member of the District ministry committee. Because Murray now believed that it would take action from outside First Church to deal with Donovan, she was ready to go directly to the District.

Murray talked with John Conner in the hope that he would be able to help her get action from the District.[2] Conner was very disturbed by the information Murray shared. At this point, his concern was more than professional: One of his relatives had also been involved with Donovan. As a member of the District ministry committee, he understood the wider ramifications of this information and also sensed the responsibility to act which lay with the District. He decided to approach Donovan directly and did so in early 1983. Donovan denied everything *and* agreed to get counseling to deal with his problem. Conner was satisfied, yet he seemed to ignore the obvious contradiction that Donovan was willing to get counseling for a problem he denied he had. Conner chose not to take the problem to the ministry committee at this time nor to discuss it with any other District leaders. He had attempted to deal with it informally; but since he had no clout to call Donovan to account for his behavior, his approach did not faze Donovan.

Even though she had dropped her membership, Marian Murray still did not give up on getting First Church to take effective action. It was now late in 1982 and First Church had a new president, Don Ivy. She told him what she knew and that she had talked to Conner. Ivy seemed very sympathetic and eager to find out more about what had been going on. He began to ask around for more information. He had been told little by the retiring president, Dan Lawson. Lawson had indicated that there had been problems, but that Donovan had received "a clean bill of health" from his psychiatrist and so Ivy should not expect further difficulties. In May 1983, Ivy talked with Barbara Preston at the annual denomination meeting. He asked a lot of questions about what she knew, and she told him as much as she felt free to tell while respecting the confidences which others had shared with her. She was amazed that he seemed to have little information from the previous president. Ivy did not know what to do with this sketchy information, and so he did nothing but worry about it.

Finally, a year later in January 1984—now three years since Murray's encounter with Donovan—she could no longer tolerate the inaction of the powers-that-be. Her sense of urgency was not shared by any of the church leaders. She had tried all the appropriate channels and gotten nowhere. She had gone to all the appropriate players: Donovan himself, both the past and current presidents of First Church, and a member of the District ministry committee; but nothing had been accomplished. She decided to go directly to the District minister, Rev. Maxwell Kelley, and appeal to him for help.[3]

This was not the first time Kelley had heard of problems with Pete Donovan; rumors had preceded Murray's visit. But this was the first concrete information that had come to him, and the first indication that a group of people was willing to talk directly with him. Joan Preston, Kristin Stone, and Marian Murray were ready to complain formally about Donovan's behavior with them. Murray assumed that Kelley would now set in motion some response from the District level to remove Donovan from First Church. Murray waited to be contacted by Kelley, but nothing happened.

In April, Nancy Linder came to Marian Murray. She told her story of Donovan's sexual relationship with her, his response to her attempt to counseling about her abusive situation. This had taken place during the previous two months, and Murray realized that Donovan was still taking advantage of women in the church. Nothing had changed; nothing effective had been done. She again contacted Maxwell Kelley and asked him how long was this going to be allowed to continue.

Concluding that the church was too slow and too ineffectual, Marian Murray began to look elsewhere for action. Because she was active in local government, she turned to county council member Jessie Sparks, an elected official. Murray knew her through the Women's Advisory Council, and believed that she would be concerned about this situation. Sparks was especially responsive to Murray's story. Her cousin had died at Jonestown, and she knew all too well the damage that a powerful, charismatic pastor could inflict. Sparks immediately called Maxwell Kelley and asked why the District had not yet acted to remove this menace from her community. It was now apparent that the "problem" Dr. Pete Donovan had created could not be kept quiet and simply be the church's secret. Kelley was very upset that a member of the county council had contacted him: It was now clear that the wider community was involved and concerned with the church's lack of effective action.

Within two weeks, Kelley met with the women and heard their stories firsthand. He was shocked and appalled; only now did he begin to comprehend the enormity of the offenses that had been perpetrated by Donovan. He assured them that he would take immediate action. It had taken two-and-a-half years to get the attention of someone with the power and the willingness to act.

Kelley said that as District minister he would meet with the council of First Church and seek Donovan's resignation.

Two weeks later, he met instead with Donovan and Don Ivy. Kelley indicated that he believed there was evidence of serious misconduct on Donovan's part, and offered Donovan the option of resignation. Kelley was attempting a pastoral intervention in the hope of avoiding a prolonged and more public official process. Enraged, Donovan denied everything; he was not about to resign. Kelley's intentions were to remove Donovan from his position and to minimize the trauma to the congregation of First Church, but his approach was inadequate. Kelley could have invoked the official proceedings of the District in response to complaints of ethical misconduct, which would have led to a hearing of the charges. This would have accomplished four things: It would have provided Donovan with due process; immediately brought the weight of the District and denomination to bear; given clear indication to the victims that they were being taken seriously; and allowed the members of First Church to be informed about what was going on. Kelley moved slowly in this direction, still hoping that Donovan's resignation would be forthcoming.

A week later, in mid-May, Maxwell Kelley met with the group of women victims and told them that he had referred the matter to the ministry committee of the District, the body officially designated to act in questions of ministerial ethics. This was the first point at which this committee was officially informed of the complaints being made about Pete Donovan. Knowing that he needed written complaints with specific allegations in order to proceed further, Kelley asked each of the women to write a letter to the District stating their complaints.

Marian Murray wrote to Maxwell Kelley, District minister, on May 16, 1984:

Dear Dr. Kelley,

It is difficult to write what must be written, but I need to share with you once again my concerns for the welfare of First Church in Newburg. It has become increasingly clear over the last couple of years that Pete Donovan should not continue to function as a Minister. His standing should be removed from the Ministry permanently because of his repeated inappropriate, immoral, unethical, deceptive and dishonest behavior.

I am appalled that the Church has not taken action any sooner to conduct an investigation of the charges that have been brought to the attention of the local Presidents. It seems that the leadership has not wanted to believe the very negative activities that have taken place. . . .

Murray then described her experience with Pete Donovan, and concluded her letter:

When I became aware of these other incidents I felt a tremendous responsibility to share them with the President in a spirit of helpfulness to the church and to the Minister as well. Some of us did that in early 1982. Soon afterwards I left the Church. It would have been hypocritical of me to support a Church that allowed him to use the Church as a platform for deception. He is indeed a scoundrel.

The multiplicity of complaints should be adequate to warrant his dismissal from the Ministry. The reputation of Ministers in general is at stake and certainly the integrity of the Church in the community is in danger. Future negative experiences must be avoided. If anyone else is harmed physically or emotionally we are all responsible. I implore you to take the action that is necessary to remove him permanently from the Ministry.

Sincerely,
Marian Murray

In her letter to the District minister, Kristin Stone wrote,

I am just the tip of the iceberg. I have spoken to six other women who have had experiences just as negative as my own, including accounts of misuse of a counseling situation. Through these other women I have become aware of many other tragic occurrences in the past two years. I am appalled that with all the lives that have been laid to waste and families that have broken up, that Pete Donovan is still allowed to abuse those inside and outside the church while "serving" as pastor.

I am one of the lucky ones. I have been able to put my life back together. What I am worried about are the younger or less stable ones. I wonder if it will take a couple of suicides before Pete is forced to resign.

Pete Donovan is a very sick man. It has been my prayer for two years that he would be forced to resign and that those silent women who have suffered so much at his hands would find wholeness and comfort in a loving God.

Stone was now ready and eager to tell her story.

When Joan Preston learned that a group of women were bringing formal complaints to the District, she sent her letter to the District office. After giving a full account of her relationship with Donovan, she concluded,

When I first realized he was seeing one other woman, I was obviously hurt—I took it personally. But when I found out he was seeing several women, I realized that I should not take it personally, because our entire relationship was not personal—I was simply one of many. After several months of hearing "rumors" about his actions, and actually observing his actions with women, now as an outsider observer, I lost all hurt, hatred and anger that I felt at first. In their place came pity for someone who does not understand or care how they hurt others—and pity for the other women who will be taken in, and hurt.

In my opinion, Pete Donovan is a detriment to First Church, and to the Christian Ministry in general.

Respect and Trust are crucial to any ministry. In his position as minister, Pete Donovan has misused this trust and respect at the expense of vulnerable women. He *must* be removed from this position immediately. . . . And further, must not be allowed access to this position of authority and trust ever again.

On May 17, 1984, Nancy Linder wrote to Dr. Maxwell Kelley. She briefly shared the particulars of her counseling relationship with Donovan, which had become a sexual relationship. She concluded, "I am concerned about the physical and emotional damage this man can do considering the vast number of women I have personally heard stories from. I cannot in all good conscience let this situation continue."

The women's words were a powerful indictment of Donovan and of the church. They were willing to give up their privacy and take whatever risks necessary to stop Donovan. Maxwell Kelley had the specifics he needed to act.

Negotiations

Don Ivy, the president of First Church, found himself in a vortex. Although he was a competent and respected administrator of a local nonprofit agency, he felt ill-prepared and isolated in dealing with this crisis at First Church. The information he had received from past president Lawson and from the women was minimal. He knew that the allegations were serious, but he never saw the women's letters or statements. He chose not to ask for that information from the women themselves because he didn't want to embarrass them further, but he also feared what he might learn. He felt there was no one in the church with whom he could sort out his feelings and consider his options.

Ivy had been handpicked by Donovan to be president, and he realized that Donovan probably expected his unquestioning loyalty. Although hesitant to confront Donovan, Ivy was not willing to play the "yes man" in light of the circumstances. Instead he became the intermediary between Donovan and the District, carrying out the negotiations.

In one conversation with Ivy, Donovan talked at length about a lesson he had learned from his grandfather. The lesson was that if you believe you are right, always keep pushing and never give up; but even if you are wrong and get caught, pick yourself up and keep pushing as though you were right, never giving up. Ivy watched as Donovan carried out this homespun strategy in the face of the ever increasing weight of official action.

Still hoping to negotiate a resignation, Maxwell Kelley met again with Donovan, Ivy, and several other layleaders from First Church. He presented Donovan with a letter requesting his voluntary resignation from First Church and from standing in the District. Kelley stated that official proceedings were in the works, and that if Donovan did not resign, formal charges would be brought resulting in an open hearing. Donovan countered with an announcement that he had been planning to resign from First Church because he felt burned out. He offered to resign November 30. This would allow him access to the pulpit and to members of the congregation, including more possible victims, for another six months. Kelley was uncomfortable and ambivalent: He felt torn between his disdain for Donovan and his belief that Donovan had brought new health, energy, and members to First Church. For the well-being of the church, Kelley was concerned that the terms of the resignation should allow Donovan time to bring adequate closure to his relationships with those members who revered him. Consequently, Kelley did not act decisively.

The efforts to negotiate with Donovan in order to get him out immediately were not succeeding. The negotiations went back and forth. One of several suggestions came from the First Church officers: Donovan would tell the congregation of his resignation on July 15 and give his last sermon on October 14; if he maintained professional standards during the next two years, no demittal action would be taken to remove his standing as a clergyperson in the denomination. Furthermore, this suggestion would require Donovan to agree not to seek employment in another church in the denomination for five years.

These terms were even less acceptable to Maxwell Kelley. His patience had run out. Kelley reported on his actions and the failed negotiations to the ministry committee. A number of reservations were raised by committee members. They were uncomfortable with the negotiations, because it appeared that something was being put over on the women victims. Someone suggested that the cleanest and quickest way for something to happen was for one of the women to file a suit against Donovan. That would have lifted some of the weight of responsibility off the shoulders of the District and passed the buck to the civil courts. It was reported that a clergywoman had been assaulted by Donovan; the committee wanted to hear from her. They were also very anxious over their suspicion that Donovan might have abused minors as well, but they did not know how to reach the families of those children and teens. They discussed the reports of threats of violence against the women who were complaining and wanted to devise some means of support for them. They concluded that it was their responsibility to act within the boundaries of the District procedures to deal with these allegations, and they were ready and willing to do so.

Rev. Ralph Bennett

Maxwell Kelley passed primary District staff responsibility to Rev. Ralph Bennett, who had been associate District minister since 1979. He had served local churches before joining the District staff, and was well known and highly regarded in the District. Bennett was conscientious and hard working; he felt a genuine concern for the people in the church as well as for the functions of the church itself. But he had never encountered anyone like Pete Donovan before. This situation presented him with issues he never expected.

Bennett first became aware of some concern about Pete Donovan in the early fall of 1980. He had heard reports from the church camp Donovan had codirected that Donovan had been "too affectionate" with some of the teenage female campers. In response to this rumor, Bennett had lunch with Donovan and told him he was concerned about his behavior with the campers. Donovan assured him there was no problem. He was just a "touching" person, and sometimes his touch was misinterpreted, but he promised to be more careful in the future.

The next information came to Bennett from Rev. Katie Simpson. In the late spring of 1981, she told Bennett that Donovan had propositioned her prior to the denomination's annual meeting in May. She wanted Bennett to be aware of what she considered to be inappropriate behavior from a colleague.

In November, six months later, Simpson had a much more specific and serious complaint to make to Bennett: She told him about the assault by Donovan in Donovan's office. But she did not give him specifics, so Bennett interpreted this as yet another inappropriate sexual proposition from Donovan. He sympathized with Simpson's frustration and sanctioned her deflection of Donovan's attention, but did nothing else.

In April 1984, two-and-a-half years later, Simpson called Ralph

Bennett and this time told him exactly what had happened. Someone had to know. Someone had to do something to prevent Pete Donovan from harming anyone else. Simpson hoped that she could trust Bennett to believe her and to act. He was sympathetic and said he understood the anxiety and agitation she was feeling. He told Maxwell Kelley about her experience. At the annual denominational meeting in early May, Kelley asked her to write and tell her story. He said that there were women from First Church who were bringing charges, and they would need Simpson's testimony. Kelley believed that a clergywoman's allegations would increase the laywomen's credibility. Simpson was glad that the District was beginning to take her seriously, but she also felt as if she was primarily a material witness in someone else's important case. Several weeks later Joe Dangerfield, another associate District minister, told Simpson how sorry he was that she had had to go through all of this with Pete Donovan. This was the first "pastoral" contact she had experienced from the District, and she was very grateful for it.

On May 22, 1984, she wrote,

Dear Maxwell,
Thank you for your efforts to end Pete Donovan's dangerous "ministry" in Newburg. Though tremendously angry and hurt, I have never told anyone of my entire experience with him. Until recently I didn't feel that anyone thought the situation was important or even believed the bits of the story that I did share. I wasn't sure who I could trust after having my trust in Pete as a colleague so violated and I have found myself trapped by all the shame, self-doubt, guilt, and confusion that sexually assaulted victims so characteristically feel. . . .

Simpson then told the whole story in her letter, and concluded,

Pete Donovan must not continue to endanger the lives of women with whom he is associated. Pete must not continue to cloak his activity in the guise of ministry in God's name. I was told that I legally couldn't prove enough to prosecute him, but at the very least his connection with our denomination must be broken. He embodies the epitome of what Christ was preaching against. I feel guilty that this experience so crippled my trust and courage that I couldn't tell the whole story long ago. And I feel

great pain and responsibility that the other women have been traumatized in these passing years.

With deep grief that I am not the only one,
The Rev. Katie Simpson

Three years after she was raped by Pete Donovan, Simpson was
finally able to tell her story to people whom she hoped could do
something about his "dangerous ministry." Looking back, she felt
as if she had told a lot of people and they had done nothing. But
in fact, not unlike victims of child molestation, she had given minimal information to a number of people who could not comprehend the gravity of her experience or do anything with what little
she told them. Nor had they sought additional information from
her. Now she was telling the whole story. At Ralph Bennett's suggestion, she joined the other women who were telling theirs.

Bennett found himself in the midst of official proceedings
brought against Dr. Pete Donovan by five laywomen from First
Church and one clergywoman. It was Bennett's job to work with
the local church and the ministry committee in response to the
complaints. His investment was twofold: Not only was this task
his responsibility as a District staff person, he also cared deeply
about the well-being of First Church and the individual women
involved. He had served First Church in the mid-sixties and knew
many of the key figures from that period of his ministry. He saw
his role as helping the District handle these allegations by using
its process for discipline. Although Bennett was genuinely worried about what had occurred, he knew that the complaints that
the District was hearing were allegations. They would need to be
proved or disproved before any action could be taken to discipline
Donovan.

On July 10, 1984, Bennett met with the six women, heard their
stories, and explained the process the ministry committee would
be following. They trusted Bennett because several of the women
knew and respected him. Although it felt like it had been a long
time coming, the women were confident that now something
would be done to stop Donovan.

As he listened to their stories, Bennett was even more convinced that the women's allegations were well-grounded. But he also knew that his job was to see the process carried out without prejudice if it was to be effective in stopping Donovan. So he worked hard to maintain a clear role for himself. He knew, however, that this would limit his ability to serve the women as a pastor. He also knew that they needed a pastor. After consulting with the ministry committee, which agreed that the women needed someone to support them through the process ahead, Bennett offered to provide an advocate and counselor. The women saw this as an effort of the District to support them through the next few months. They were cautious but willing. Bennett called me and I responded.

Bennett asked me to serve as an advocate for the women, to assist them in preparing their complaints, and to be pastor to them in this crisis. These things I was prepared and willing to do. But I sensed that the staff and committee had an unstated expectation: They hoped I would assess the stability of the women and the validity of their stories. That was the responsibility of the ministry committee, and I disregarded it. On July 16, I met with the women. Afterward, I had no reason to question the veracity of their reports. I had no hesitation in advocating for them. As we began to know each other, they began to trust me. I saw my job as listening to their experience and providing them with information and support, which gave them a firm foundation from which to stand together in this complaint process. My goal was to do whatever I could to assure them of just treatment in the face of their victimization. I felt this was the best I could do as their pastor.

Policies and Procedures: A Modest Critique

The District's policies and procedures related to the misconduct of a pastor were only rarely used to discipline clergy. The District staff and ministry committee quickly discovered that these procedures were not adequate to address the problem before them. The procedures were introduced by the following paragraph:

In matters where ministerial character is called into question by charges of professional incompetence, financial irresponsibilty, moral turpitude, criminal behavior, or other breach of ministerial ethics, the minister in question is urged to seek the help of the District Minister. Such charges may be brought in writing, to the attention of the Ministry Committee by the minister in question, by the District Minister, by the local church in which the minister holds membership, or by an Association Moderator. The Ministry Committee, upon receipt of such charges from any of these sources, shall do the following. . . .

According to the steps that follow, the committee's first responsibility is to attempt to clear the reputation of the pastor. When that is not possible, the committee is to set up an adjudication process so that all people involved receive due process. If the process determines that the minister "has brought dishonor on himself or herself and the ministerial calling," the committee shall recommend to the board of directors of the District that the pastor's standing be "revoked for cause." If it finds that the minister has been wrongly accused, the committee shall do all it can to clear his or her name. If the accused pastor refuses to participate in the adjudication process, the committee may recommend to the board that his or her standing be suspended pending cooperation. Continued refusal to cooperate, "coupled with the weight of responsible evidence may compel" the committee to recommend loss of standing with prejudice. A formal appeal of findings could be made through the District board of directors.

The main difficulty the District faced in trying to follow this process was that it found here only an outline of what needed to be done. Although the outline provided for the basics of (1) formal, written complaints, (2) an adjudication process through a hearing, and (3) the empowerment of the committee and board to act on its findings, the lack of detailed direction quickly became an issue. The attorney who sat on the committee also raised questions about the legality of the process; he feared the accused might have grounds for a civil suit against the District.

The shortcomings of the procedures were numerous. Nowhere was there a definition of "moral turpitude." Nowhere was there a statement that sexual contact with parishioners or counselees by the pastor was unethical and unprofessional. This vagueness is not unusual in references to clergy ethics; nonetheless, it left the committee in limbo in simply determining that the charges, if they were founded, constituted "moral turpitude."[4]

In addition, there was no provision in the process for an individual directly affected by a minister's misconduct to bring forth a complaint. It had to be brought by the District staff, denominational leadership, or local church leadership. This meant that an individual layperson did not really have access to the official process unless she or he could first convince the local church or denominational leadership to bring the complaint. As Marian Murray discovered, after getting no support from the lay leaders of First Church, she finally had to go to the District minister, who eventually involved the ministry committee.

The procedures never mentioned the need to inform the local church members about the charges or the process to deal with them. Don Ivy and the other officers had been closely involved; but there was no indication to the members of First Church that their pastor had been charged with unethical conduct, was being investigated, and that his standing in the denomination was in jeopardy. Needless to say, rumors had begun to fly. But the lack of formal notice to the church prevented church members from realizing the seriousness of the charges, and allowed Donovan to rally his supporters in response to what he painted as harassment by the District. The lack of notice also contributed to the scapegoating of those who had brought complaints. Many people concluded that the women were the source of the problem. They became isolated and stigmatized as the rumor mill worked overtime.

Ethically, the procedures raised significant issues. The first priority laid out was to protect the minister's reputation. At no point is the need to advocate for the complainants/victims and to seek justice for them stated as a priority of the process. Because false charges are always a possibility, the minister's rights to due process, fair treatment, and a defense must be protected. But the primary purpose of the process should be to hear complaints, judge their veracity, adjudicate, and then discipline the pastor when necessary in order to protect the members of the church from the consequences of misconduct. Only these unequivocal steps can protect the credibility of the pastoral office and bring healing to the individual victims and the church.

The weight of the institution should have been brought to bear in a formal accountability process from the very beginning. The early pastoral intervention and warnings by the First Church president and by the District minister did not work because of their informality. When a minister like Donovan behaves unethically and the authorities merely express concern and issue a warning, he is likely to be more discreet in the future but not likely to change his behavior. There were no negative consequences in this approach and no clear determination that his behavior was unacceptable in the ministry. Hence there was little impact on Donovan.

The negotiation process which became the focus of the District's response was never part of the stated procedures: They literally made it up as they went along. Although it was intended to bring about a speedy resolution to the matter, it effectively avoided the important steps everyone needed. This was not a conflict between individuals in the church that called for mediation and a negotiated settlement.[5] One person's behavior had caused harm to others, to the church, and to the profession of the ministry. The process should not have been to seek to negotiate or to resolve a conflict between parties, but to advocate for those harmed and to call the offending party to account. In this situation, the church as institution had to take sides with those harmed when it became apparent that harm had been done.

For everyone involved, the negotiation process became an effort to circumvent official proceedings. The District leadership thought negotiation was to their advantage, because they believed it would hasten Donovan's removal and would protect the reputation of First Church. Donovan used the negotiations to maintain his control over the process and to avoid an open hearing in which damning information would become public. But once it was clear that individuals were making formal complaints and were willing to come forward with them, Donovan should have been suspended with salary pending an investigation of the charges. This action would have accomplished several things: (1) it would have placed the control of the process with the ministry committee and the District rather than with Donovan; (2) it would have disallowed Donovan access to the pulpit and to future victims in First Church; (3) it would have clearly indicated the seriousness of the matter and the commitment of the District to act; and (4) it would have been the best insurance that Donovan would have a fair hearing. Then, following the gathering of necessary information, a formal hearing should have been scheduled.

The Committee Hears the Women and Donovan

On July 20, the ministry committee met with each of the six complainants in an informal hearing. The women carefully and painstakingly told their stories. Several of the women commented on their fear of Donovan. Each of the women recalled Donovan's verbal harangues. One said that he would yell at her over the phone; another recalled that he would get purple with anger. One had heard that he had gone after another woman with a baseball bat, and ever since she had been afraid that he would hit her when he was angry. Marian Murray began her comments to the committee by saying, "I might not have believed the stories had I not had a personal experience with him myself." As the particulars of each story unfolded, the picture became clearer. Although each woman was different in age and circumstance, Donovan's pattern was similar in all cases: an emotional and sexual come-on, a requirement of secrecy, and a promise of a special, unique relationship; when there was resistance to his sexual approach, he used force to overcome it.

Pete Donovan also met with the ministry committee that day. They reviewed the process with Donovan and the nature of the allegations, as well as the committee's assessment that there was sufficient evidence to proceed with a hearing. Donovan's response was agitated and disjointed. Initially, he acknowledged that he had had sex with some women in the congregation, but it was never in a counseling situation and he never forced anyone against her will. He was anxious to know whether the complaints were all hearsay or whether people were bringing direct testimony, and if anyone was planning to bring criminal charges against him.

This meeting may have been the first time Donovan realized he was in serious trouble. His speech was rambling and confusing, a mixture of denial and acknowledgment heavily interspersed with his assertion that this was all a conspiracy to get him. This was the beginning of Donovan's "I am the victim here" strategy. But, in the eyes of the committee, the irrational nature of Donovan's conversation only served to support further the women's allegations.

Donovan expounded at length on his theory of a conspiracy by the women involved: "I never did figure out the motive, but it became important to them to get me. This is well orchestrated. If they met and talked with each other in an attempt to get their stories straight, then this smells like conspiracy. I see this for what it is: For some peculiar reason, these people are out to get me." He vehemently denied the charges: "I have never, never treated anybody this way. It's my word against theirs. I don't have to force anybody to have sexual relations. I've never had anyone fight me off. I did go out with women in the church, and that was a stupid mistake. But I've been a good minister; I've done a good job. But I'm bored as a minister." A stunned silence fell over the meeting.

Uncertain how to respond, one of the committee members commented, "I believe that you believe that you didn't do these things. I wonder if you are distorting what happened." Donovan replied, "You mean in my own head? Yes, I've thought about this. The only thing I am weighing is if I am crazy. But what if I am innocent?" Someone put forth a suggestion: "What about resignation with prejudice on the basis of the allegation of sexual contact with parishioners?" Donovan's response was quick and pointed. "Either I'm going to be proven guilty, or I'm going to be absolved, or I'm going to resign my standing with the agreement that my file be locked in the District office." He angrily dug in his heels.

Then someone said to Donovan, "You seem very angry. Are you planning to withdraw First Church from the District?" He returned to the conspiracy discussion, this time focusing on the District minister, Maxwell Kelley: "You want to know why I am taking the church out of the District? Because Maxwell Kelley went behind my back in secret meetings with the church officers. I know he met with Dan Lawson and Harvey Johnson and with Barbara Preston. He also met with Dan and Don Ivy." He had attended this last meeting: It was the occasion when he offered his resignation as of November 30. Turning on the committee, Donovan said, "I know you're working for the District. I know whose side you're on." This accusation was partially accurate: The committee *was* delegated by the District to deal with allegations of ministerial misconduct and to seek some just and fair resolution of this situation.

As the discussion deteriorated into a question of who was out to get whom, the committee chairperson posed the options to Donovan: "You can either voluntarily resign your standing in the District or go through the hearing process which, if you are found guilty of the charges, will also result in your loss of standing." He replied, "I will resign from First Church on November 30 and the congregation may then want to rehire me. If I am going to be a victim, I haven't even started fighting yet. I was a good minister and I still am. I have worked hard." Another member pressed the question of his responsibility: "I believe that you believe you are innocent. My questions revolve around whether you gave inappropriate attentions to these women. Are you open to the possibility that inadvertently you crossed over some lines?" This seemed to bring Donovan as close to acknowledgment as he would come: "Of course. Many of us have done that. But I never forced anyone. I saw a psychiatrist because I didn't want to pursue this whole thing without a good look at my past. I really need help badly. I swear to God I didn't do these things. If I did these things, help me. Take your time before you throw this into a public meeting. I have never taken advantage of anyone who came to me for counseling. Oh, I probably have, but . . . I am sure that I have played lots of roles and one of those roles may have been that I was being seductive. I needed psychiatric help; I didn't want to be unprofessional. I should get myself to talk with someone about this. But if there are names other than Preston, Murray, Mitchell, Rogers, Jasper, and Saxton, then I have a problem. If it is just those people, then I will fight it." Donovan had failed to name Kristin Stone, Katie Simpson, and Nancy Linder. But he had just named three additional women who had not yet come forward. He was right. He did have a problem.

Finally, the committee met with the officers from First Church. Again the summary of charges was provided, and the options of action were laid out: a formal hearing before the committee, or a negotiated settlement for voluntary resignation with prejudice.

Being faced with these options left the officers of First Church in an awkward position. It seemed unclear as to what next steps needed to be taken and by whom. The committee preferred the voluntary resignation route, and seemed to be asking the officers to intercede with Donovan to persuade him to accept voluntary resignation. The possibility of the hearing was the weight they held over Donovan's head. Yet in fact the officers and congregation together were the only body that could fire Donovan from First Church, and the ministry committee (by recommendation to the board of directors) was the only body that could remove Donovan's standing. Since both groups were trying to avoid an open hearing process, they continued to negotiate with a person with whom they should not have been negotiating.

Some of the First Church officers were concerned that although rumors were rife, only a few members of the congregation knew what was going on. No one was willing to tell them. The result was very divisive. The officers realized that this lack of information was not helping First Church; and they, too, were feeling the heat of the rumors that "the leadership" (which now included them) was "out to get Donovan." They could not act until the committee finished its work: The local church leadership felt powerless until someone had adjudicated the charges. But the District passed the responsibility back to them to get Donovan simply to resign. The common effort to circumvent the hearing continued to lead all the players around in circles.

At no point in this discussion with the First Church officers did any of them defend Donovan or challenge the validity of the allegations. One of First Church's officers pressed further: What if *prima facie* (that is, evidence sufficient to establish a fact) evidence of rape appeared? Would the effort to negotiate continue or would this move the committee to action? The committee hedged that question by saying that they were only responsible for the question of Donovan's standing; criminal complaints would need to be brought to the district attorney by the women. The exception would be any evidence of *statutory* rape; then the committee would go directly to the district attorney. The First Church officers were trying to press the question of the seriousness of the charges: If the charges were very serious and there was clearly sufficient evidence, shouldn't the committee give up the negotiations and use the hearing process to remove Donovan's standing? The officers wanted the District to act. The committee hesitated again, still trying to avoid a hearing.

The final outcome of this long committee meeting was to ask the women complainants to standardize the format of their written complaints. Each was to cover the same points of information: who, what, when, where, and so forth. The committee's intention was to get the material into a final, organized form with which they could work. But for the women, this was the fourth time they had to recount their stories. They were confused and perturbed, but agreed because they were convinced it would help.

So Close and Yet So Far

On July 28, 1984, I met again with Marian Murray, Bernie Mitchell, Kristin Stone, Katie Simpson, Nancy Linder, and Barbara Preston. After dinner, each woman who had been victimized sat and painstakingly wrote once again of her experience. Joan

Preston's statement followed later. I had asked each to prepare her statement in six categories:

1. Nature of your relationship with Donovan (employee, counselee, church member, colleague, etc.).
2. Nature of encounter preceding sexual contact (who approached whom and for what purpose?).
3. Nature of sexual contact (verbal suggestions, fondling, intercourse, etc.).
4. Reaction—how did you feel? what did you do? (consent, comply, resist, etc.).
5. Was there a request for secrecy from Donovan?
6. Have you been threatened in any way? specify.

Their responses within this framework resulted in six complaints, which provided consistent categories of information for the committee.

In a cover letter that accompanied the complaints, I summarized the allegations of unethical conduct:

• Peter Donovan suggested, initiated or carried out sexual contact with persons subordinate to him, i.e., counselees and employees, on at least 14 occasions. The contact included kissing, fondling, and sexual intercourse.

• Peter Donovan misused the power and authority of his ministerial office to manipulate, coerce or intimidate parishioners on at least 7 occasions. These included giving promises of marriage, use of abusive and profane language regarding church members, threats of retaliation, and misrepresentation.

• Peter Donovan used verbal threats to intimidate individuals and keep them from reporting his conduct to the appropriate bodies on at least 3 occasions.

• Peter Donovan used overt physical force to overcome resistance and force sexual intercourse with individuals on at least 4 occasions.

The formal complaints were sent to the District on July 30, 1984. At this point, the women felt strongly that they did not want the information in the formal complaints released to anyone without their authorization. They feared both Donovan's misuse of the particulars in a public setting and his possible retaliation. Since it was not clear whether Donovan knew exactly who all the women complainants were, they wanted to conceal themselves from him as long as possible. They also began to realize that they needed a bargaining chip in this negotiation process. Their final, formal statements provided that leverage.

I suggested to Ralph Bennett that the signed individual statements be kept confidential for the time being, but that a listing of the specific charges without names be given immediately to Donovan in order to make clear the seriousness of the complaints. Then, one week prior to a hearing date, the statements themselves could be given to Donovan in order for him to prepare his defense.

As the committee reviewed the formal charges, they felt that they had sufficient information to support the women's allegations and that in all probability, other women had been harmed. The committee was now convinced that Donovan was out of control and dangerous. Their goals became clearer: quickly remove Pete Donovan from First Church, and insure that he would not again serve a church in this denomination. They were very concerned that Donovan still had access to a pulpit each Sunday, as well as frequent contact in counseling with members of the congregation. While defaming the women complainants in meetings, Donovan was mobilizing support among the current First Church members and he was still threatening to pull the congregation out of the District. Regardless of whether he could have engineered this secession, the committee took his threat seriously. Still they pressed for voluntary resignation in the hope of accomplishing their goals.

Several days later, the women met with Ralph Bennett to discuss the terms of negotiation with Donovan. Even though Bennett believed that Donovan was guilty and should lose his standing immediately, he attempted to play a middle role in order to bring about a speedy resolution. His heart was with the women and their anguish, but his responsibility as he saw it remained elsewhere. He began to lose credibility with the women.

Bennett proposed to the women that their statements be given to Donovan, that Donovan agree to resign immediately, that all records be sealed, and that no one speak publicly about these events. The women agreed with one major exception: They wanted the district to send a letter immediately to each member of First Church stating the charges and the negotiated settlement resulting in Donovan's resignation. This letter would be the first official information that would go to the congregation. The women were deeply concerned for First Church and its future and they believed that the members deserved to know what was going on. They also knew intuitively that this information was their only protection. Rumors had already minimized the seriousness of the abuse, blamed them for creating this problem and tarnishing the reputation of the pastor and the church, and ostracized them from the community. Most people did not know the accusations Donovan was facing, nor how convincing the women's testimony was.

On August 6, 1984, a letter was delivered to Donovan outlining the categories of charges against him, the names of the women bringing the charges, and a summary of the process that would be followed from here on out:

Upon receipt of this letter containing the charges and the names of the women bringing the charges, a process is initiated which will move to a formal hearing before the Ministry Committee. September 14, 1984, has been set for this hearing. As stated in the District Manual on Ministry, "Where the minister has been shown to have brought dishonor on himself or herself and the ministerial calling, the committee will, by a ⅔ or more vote of the total committee present, vote to recommend to the Board of Directors that ministerial standing be revoked for cause. The action of the Board of Directors may result in loss of ministerial standing. The loss of standing means this person is no longer recognized by the District as one who should be supported or recommended as a professional clergyperson. This person also loses the privilege to vote at District meetings.

If the minister has proved to have been wronged by such charges, the Ministry Committee shall endeavor to make public its adjudication in every area where such charges have been raised."

As you will recall from your meeting with the Ministry Committee you may, if you choose, avoid the full hearing process at any time through a voluntary permanent resignation of ministerial standing.

If you choose voluntary permanent resignation of standing within the next 36 hours, a letter will be sent to all concerned parties, including the members of First Church of Newburg, stating the fact and the terms as negotiated and approved by the Ministry Committee.

If you choose to move toward the hearing with the Ministry Committee on the charges, a letter will be sent to all concerned parties, including the members of First Church of Newburg, informing them of the charges and of the hearing process.

It is important that, in light of the seriousness of the charges, and of the orderly process through which they are being handled, and the perception of the women that you may seek to intimidate or threaten them in some way, that any contact with any of the persons whose names are attached to the charges be made through your attorney. Personal contact could be perceived to be intimidation, and therefore serve as the basis of other charges in itself.

The Ministry Committee is charged with assuring that all parties in this situation are treated with all fairness and compassion our faith requires, and we want to assure you of our willingness to be of any assistance to you during the extremely stressful and difficult time.

Attached to the letter were the individual statements from the women bringing the charges.

Key to Donovan's options, as outlined here, was the fact that he could voluntarily resign and avoid a hearing or proceed with the hearing process; either way, a letter would go to the congregation explaining the nature of the charges and the resolution of the matter. The women had agreed that their individual statements could be released to Donovan if the informational letter were sent to the congregation. They were willing to give up their privacy in order to insure that the congregation know what had happened. Bennett and the committee agreed; they too wanted some means to inform the congregation fully.

A Promise Betrayed

Three days later, on August 9, Don Ivy, president of First Church, called Bennett and reported that Donovan was ready to resign his standing but unwilling to have any letter go to the congregation. If the letter were to go out, Donovan refused to resign and threatened again to withdraw the congregation from the denomination.[6] He said he wanted to go to the hearing in order "to tell the truth about those women"; he may even have believed that he could be vindicated. Donovan certainly did not want that letter to go out. Without that official information from the District to First Church, he was able to deliver to members of the congregation his unchallenged version of the alleged events. He wanted to complete his tenure at First Church playing the victim of unjust and malicious gossip. So he called the District's hand, betting that the District was eager to get him out quickly and that it feared his potential to lead First Church away from the denomination. His gamble paid off. The District was stampeded into a premature deal which, in the end, benefited only Donovan and betrayed their commitment to the women.[7]

Bennett compromised on the letter to the congregation. In exchange for Donovan's speedy resignation (his last Sunday would be August 26) and an end to his attempt to withdraw First Church from the denomination, Bennett agreed that no communication about the specifics of the charges would go to the congregation. But he held out for a letter to be sent after Donovan left, outlining the process which had taken place. He believed that it was more imperative to get Donovan out before he did any more damage than to keep the commitment to the women. A hearing would have left Donovan at First Church for at least six months. In addition, Bennett agreed to Donovan's request that all District records of the case be sealed and that none of the principals (Donovan, the women, the First Church officers, and the denominational leaders) involved be able to speak about what had transpired.

The First Church officers agreed to the compromise because they wanted to minimize the information that would have gone to the congregation and to avoid the embarrassment this would cause for the church in the community. Donovan pressed for the compromise because he did not want any information shared that would erode his credibility any further. Bennett and the committee realized in retrospect that they had allowed the absence of a provision for suspending the accused during the investigation and the lack of a mandatory hearing to tie their hands. They wanted Donovan out immediately, so they decided to cut their losses and agree to his terms. Unfortunately, this judgment call would exact a high and long-lasting price.

The women were never consulted about the final compromise. Bennett bound them to silence without their consent. From their perspective, he gave away a great deal, including the congregation's right to know and their right to speak publicly about what was happening. They were angry and felt betrayed by Bennett and the District. Even though Bennett tried to convince them of the value of this compromise, they felt that the one thing they most wanted had been sacrificed. Once again Donovan was in control: His terms had been met and his reputation was being protected, while the needs of the women and First Church were abandoned.

The compromise betrayed not only the women but also First Church. Notifying the local congregation about the serious complaints should never have been negotiable. The congregation was denied the opportunity to face the facts. Other victims of Donovan's misconduct were still in the congregation. The lack of information and involvement of the congregation in the process left them isolated and afraid. The body, the church family, was closing ranks. Out of their ignorance and fear, many members were unable to respond to the pain of the victims and to the need for responsible action, so they were easy prey to Donovan's continuing deceptions and manipulation. The one thing that would have helped them, even though it would have heightened their pain at first, was to have been informed about all that was taking place.

The women believed that they had patiently given the system a chance to right a wrong done to them, and now the system had failed at the most critical juncture. Up until now they had been satisfied to rely on the institutional church to respond, even though imperfectly, to their victimization. They were no longer satisfied. The alternative institution to which they looked was the legal system. Perhaps a civil suit could provide justice, prevent Donovan from continuing to have access to people as a pastor, and give the members of the congregation the information they needed. At this point, they knew that they had been harmed by Donovan, they knew that First Church had been negligent in not dealing with this problem earlier, and they now felt that the District had betrayed their interests. A suit should be brought against all three parties.

They discussed this option for a long time. Their feelings pulled them in many directions and they were not of one mind. They were looking for justice, and for months it had been deferred. They were never vengeful, but they were angry. They wanted to sue Donovan in the hope that a substantial financial penalty would deter his criminal behavior. Although they agreed that both First Church and the District had been negligent in taking action to stop Donovan, they knew that some people within both bodies had worked hard on their behalf, and they did not want to hurt them. They also still had a love for the church, even though it had been sorely tested. Because of their mixed feelings about the church's role and its ineffectiveness, they could not agree on the pursuit of civil litigation. However, they did agree that they would still have to go outside of the church in order to call the church to accountability.

The Secrecy Is Broken

The women wanted public disclosure of the charges against Donovan. Surprisingly, they felt bound to silence by the agreement Bennett had made for them. But there were others who were not bound by this agreement. Someone outside the church, who knew the details and had access to the media, offered to leak the story to the press. The women knew it was a gamble, but they believed it was worth the risk in order to get information to the members of First Church. They gave their consent and then they waited.

Events moved quickly. On August 15, Rev. Katie Simpson, the clergywoman who brought a complaint, returned home from work to find a whispered message on her tape machine: "I'm going to kill you." She was certain that it was Donovan's voice. She and her husband took the tape to the Newburg police. She spent three hours telling her story. At this point, the police couldn't do anything about the 1981 assault: The law at that time did not consider what was done to Simpson to be rape. They would not consider it attempted rape, because they said Simpson could not prove that Donovan's intention was to rape. (The state law was changed in late 1981 to define rape as penetration of the vagina by any object against the will of the victim.) More important was the fact that since she did not report it immediately to the police and had no witnesses, the district attorney felt that he could not effectively file charges. However, the police were worried about the death threat and took it seriously. They advised her to take precautions and to notify them immediately if Donovan had any further contact with her. Others of the women had seen Donovan driving around their neighborhoods at odd hours, and they received phone calls from someone who would not speak and then hang up. They were becoming unnerved and fearful, afraid to stay alone in their homes at night. They began to develop contingency safety plans with each other. They did not know what Donovan would do, but they feared the worst.

In the meantime, on August 17, Donovan met with the ministry committee to accept formally the terms of his resignation from First Church and to give up his standing in the District. It was agreed that the records would be sealed until or unless he again sought standing in the denomination (in this or any District) or a civil or criminal action was brought forth. Donovan could no longer serve as an ordained minister in this denomination, but it did not remove his ordination *per se* so that he remained a minister. The committee also informed him that a letter would go to all the districts of the denomination, alerting them that he had voluntarily resigned but with prejudice. This was the one action Bennett had insisted on to warn other districts in case Donovan simply tried to move and start over. This letter insured that if he requested standing in another District, they would be alert to request information; at that point, the files would be opened. On August 18, the District board of directors voted to accept Dr. Peter Donovan's voluntary, permanent resignation of standing as a minister in the denomination.

The fact that the files were sealed, that the complainants, District staff, and First Church officers were bound not to discuss the specifics of the charges in public, and that there would be no hearing meant that there would be little opportunity for the members of First Church to understand what had happened and why. Yet Donovan was free to deny any and all allegations. His supporters rallied around a man whom they saw as a victim of malicious gossip. Those who were not so supportive remained puzzled, confused, and hurt by what they heard.

On August 24, two days before Donovan's last day at First Church, the media broke the story. Local television, radio, and newspapers carried the story of Donovan's resignation and of the nature of the charges brought against him by the women. Headlines such as "Resignation Splits Newburg Congregation," "Newburg Church Sex Case Dropped," "Resigned Minister Won't Face Charges," and "Pastor Resigns in Wake of Sex Charges" greeted the local community and First Church members. The secret had now been at least partially broken. Several investigative journalists presented the history of Donovan's ministry and the questions about his conduct as far back as his previous pastorate. The reports indicated that Donovan was now facing charges of "moral turpitude and ministerial misconduct" related to sexual misconduct with women parishioners whom he had counseled. The actual substance of the individual complaints was still not revealed.

The women victims still felt compelled not to make direct statements to the press, but Donovan felt no such qualms. He responded willingly to their inquiries and used the forum to deny the allegations vehemently and to defame the women who brought them: "I'm not the first minister to have been accused of something like this by gossips." He attributed his resignation to "professional burnout." Likewise, First Church moderator Don Ivy called the complaints "verbiage" and said that most of the members of First Church held their pastor in "very, very high esteem for his leadership and many other qualities."[8] Bennett and the committee refused to make more than general statements to the press. Even so, enough information was included to alert First Church and Newburg to the scope of the problem.

Many members of the congregation were horrified: some because of the embarrassment of public disclosure of information they were certain was untrue, but others because for the first time they began to realize how serious this matter really was. The consequence was a backlash from many First Church members. They were angry that their church's dirty laundry was being aired for all to see and they were angry that they had not been told before reading it in the paper. Many church members turned their distress again toward the women who were, in the minds of many, the source of the problem, the publicity, and the pain that now faced First Church.

The next day, Donovan met with his supporters at the church. He upheld part of the bargain and urged his supporters to remain in the denomination, to support the lay leadership of Don Ivy, and to move toward healing the pain that this episode had caused them. Seeming magnanimous, he carried his role of the unjustly accused to the very end.

The following day was Donovan's last Sunday at First Church. It was to be an extravaganza of farewell and happy birthday as he turned forty. A local Monday morning newspaper article reported the event. It referred to Donovan's resignation "under a cloud of allegations about sexual misconduct" without naming any specifics. Church members were described as disturbed that someone whom they respected as their pastor was being "forced out" by "a few troublemakers." Donovan, appearing untouched by the uproar, preached his last sermon titled, "Hello . . . Goodbye . . ." This sermon on the theme that "people should look for 'the miracle' in each other" was, according to one member present, the same sermon he preached on his first Sunday at First Church of Newburg over four years ago.

At the conclusion, most of the overflow crowd gave him a standing ovation which seemed to touch him. He left immediately avoiding the fortieth birthday party waiting for him in the church hall. Here members holding hands and weeping sang, "You Light Up My Life."

In his parting words from the pulpit, Donovan thanked his friends for the letters and calls of support he had been receiving and said, "Suffice it to say, I think that after nearly five years, and I look around this room, well—I know who I am. And I know that you know who I am."

Unfortunately, most of the church members who attended this last Sunday sevice did not know who Peter Donovan was. By controlling the disciplinary process and refusing an open hearing, Donovan had been able to maintain the charade of his ministry and hold on to the support of many of the First Church parishioners who rallied to his defense. Thus he left this senior pastorate as the poor, maligned victim of gossip put forth by a small group of perennial troublemakers. He still had the congregation in the palm of his hand and he sought all the sympathy he could get. All that most of the parishioners knew at this point was what they had read in the papers and even here the allegations were still vague. But what little they read about charges of "moral turpitude and other breaches of ministerial ethics" was unbelievable to many of them, so they chose not to believe it. Instead, most simply denied that there was any basis for the complaints, while others minimized the accusations against their bachelor pastor: "He's been the biggest catch in town; he's intelligent and all the members have been after him."

The congregation that morning was composed predominantly of his staunch supporters, a few who were uncertain, and at least one who was there to see what happened: Barbara Preston wanted to know firsthand how Donovan handled his departure. None of the other women who had been involved in the complaints attended. Many people knew that Preston had spoken out about Donovan's behavior and had fully supported her daughter, Joan, in her allegations against him. When services concluded, Preston stepped outside the building. There the television crews and reporters waited to interview members. Some of the members angrily turned on Preston and screamed at her: "You should be stoned. How could you bring this disgrace on our church?" Some yelled at her to get out of the church; others shouted to "cast out the devils." Several pushed toward her and she was visibly shaken and afraid. Preston was not even one of the complainants, and yet, as their supporter, this was the treatment that she received in the midst of Donovan's farewell party. That evening the local news programs revealed to their viewers the open hostility toward the victims which had poured forth from First Church. They were seeing the phenomenon of "shooting the messenger who brings the bad news." Still Donovan was untouched. The women and their supporters, not Donovan, were seen as the cause of all this disturbance.

Underlying the congregation's anger was their grief at the loss of a pastor whom they loved and admired. But somewhere in the recesses of their minds was also a nagging question: What if there was some truth to these vague accusations? To have believed that there was some cause for concern, some basis for the charges being brought would have required many First Church members completely to reassess their view of their minister and acknowledge that they too had been betrayed by him. Only a few were courageous enough to do this. He had meant too much to many of them. On this day of celebration and sad farewell, most could not face that possibility.

Two days later, on August 28, it was not any easier. An evening meeting was held for all First Church members in order to hear the details of the process the ministry committee had followed in dealing with the complaints against Donovan. Bennett made the statement for the District. Maxwell Kelley, the District minister, and members of the ministry committee attended. I was also present and was introduced as the counselor for the women. The press were well represented. The mood of the group that night was tense and expectant. The murmuring before the meeting began was anxious and purposeful, not the usual casual chatter.

The church president, Don Ivy, spoke first. Ivy acknowledged that many people in the congregation were hurting upon finding out that one whom they admired so much may have engaged in misconduct. He said that specific charges and allegations would not be discussed, but that they fell under the categories of "moral turpitude and breach of ministerial ethics." He asked those in the meeting not to request details, and explained that this was to protect those who brought the allegations. In fact, it was only to protect Donovan; those who had brought the allegations wanted the congregation to have all the information.

Bennett attempted to describe the process chronologically in order to convince the group that the actions the church had taken were fair. He said as much as he could and still honor his agreement with Donovan not to discuss the particulars. He summarized the procedures thus far: Allegations of misconduct had been brought in writing by six women. The allegations were investigated and clarified. The committee met with the women, the officers at First Church, and Donovan. Bennett emphasized that the goal of the process was to clear a minister's name and reestablish the well-being of the congregation if possible. If it was not possible to clear the pastor, then they would proceed with a hearing process. He then delineated the agreement that had been made with Donovan, which included his voluntary resignation from standing in the District, his resignation from First Church, the sealing of his file, and silence on the specific charges. Many were upset that Donovan had not been given a chance to defend himself against the charges. Bennett agreed that it was unfortunate that no official judgment as to guilt or innocence could be made. But he made it very clear that this was because Donovan avoided an open hearing by voluntarily resigning. It was Donovan's choice, not the District's, that the process be cut short.

The meeting was heated and emotional. People were anxious and some were visibly hostile. The most vocal members were Donovan's supporters, who did not hesitate to lambaste the District for meddling in their affairs and trying to ruin Donovan's reputation. But a significant number among the hundred who attended sat very quietly. They wanted information they had heretofore been denied, and they were clearly hearing some things for the first time.

Ivy wanted to avoid discussion as much as possible. Bennett was bound by his agreement with Donovan not to reveal the specifics of the charges. The group was floundering in its confusion and frustration. Many of them did not understand what the big issue was, because they did not know what Donovan had done. And no one would tell them. The secret was maintained, and now the people suffering the most were the members of the congregation. It is no surprise that they turned their disappointment, disbelief, and anger toward the District. Donovan remained largely untouched, and the congregation was denied an opportunity to grieve and be angry with Donovan.

Clearly no support was forthcoming for the women. No one at this meeting acknowledged the women's pain or victimization. When I was introduced as their counselor and pastor, the response was that the District had unfairly stacked the deck against Donovan by bringing in this outsider to assist the women. Ironically, if anyone could have spoken clearly that night about the nature of the charges, I could have. I was not bound by any agreement with Donovan; and the women had given me permission to share any part of their stories I felt would be of help to others. I weighed the costs and benefits of taking the floor and delineating the charges. I wanted the members of First Church to have the information I believed they needed, and I wanted them to feel some empathy for the women. But, in the midst of this heightened hostility, I feared that listing the charges against Donovan—which included rape—would only serve to increase their rage against the women.[9] Yet I could have given voice to the victims who were not present. I did not speak. I doubt that I would make the same decision again. Knowing what I know now, I would take the chance of being misheard and misunderstood, because I believe it is wrong for victims to be silenced as these women were.

The meeting closed with feelings very raw. Nothing was resolved and little was accomplished. We had gone through the motions of informing the congregation as to why their pastor had abruptly resigned, but we had not given all of them what they needed. On the way to the parking lot, some of the members of First Church were finally beginning to realize that the charges were true and that they too had been betrayed by their pastor. They began to realize the seriousness of the situation and were concerned for the women's well-being. Sadly, they did not know how to convey their feelings to the women.

Another Victim

As the meeting broke up, I stood by and talked with several reporters and committee members. A woman named Sally Jackson took me aside and said that she knew exactly what these women had been through and asked me to call her. I called her the next day and simply listened.

Jackson said that she wished she had been brave enough to speak at the meeting. The story she told was the same as all the others, only her experience with Donovan had taken place just weeks before. Even at the height of the drama of investigation and confrontation, Donovan was still preying on his parishioners. She had become friends with Donovan through the church early in August. When she heard that Donovan was getting married, she went to see him to wish him well. At the end of this brief conversation, Donovan passionately embraced and kissed her. Then she started getting phone calls from Donovan pressing her to see him. Jackson resisted Donovan's advances from the beginning. She told him that he scared her and that she did not want to do anything to hurt her husband and family; she couldn't believe that he, a pastor, would do this with a married woman. Feeling intimidated, she accepted his calls for several weeks because she did not know what else to do. When she read the newspaper on August 24, she realized what was happening to her. Even between the lines she knew that she was now in the same situation as these women who had made complaints to the District. She called Donovan, read the article to him over the phone, and told him she did not want to see him again.

Jackson said that she felt cheated and used, but she also felt stupid for not realizing what was happening sooner. She went to the meeting the night before in order to get more information. She said that she wished she could have spoken up and explained to the congregation how these things happen, but she was afraid and embarrassed. She just wanted Donovan to go away. Now that the secret was revealed, she was willing to come forward. Her anger propelled her to speak up. She expressed gratitude to the women and to the District for bringing it out in the open before something even more damaging occurred.

Hearing Jackson's story was the final straw for Bennett. When the official process had begun, Donovan had promised Bennett that he would cease counseling or meeting with individual women from church. Donovan had assured him that during those two months he had not done anything that could be construed as inappropriate. Yet here was one of his most recent victims, whom he had approached in August. Bennett now realized that Donovan had continued his misconduct with total disregard for the proceedings in which they were engaged. Bennett felt the betrayal personally. His patience, which he had struggled to maintain in order to keep faith with the process, finally gave out and his anger burst forth. He was now convinced that Donovan was dangerous to those around him and a disgrace to the ministry.

The Aftermath

During this same week, the local papers reported that two women had filed criminal complaints against Donovan with the police. Rev. Katie Simpson and Kristin Stone had gone to the police because their experiences were in fact forcible rape and because they were less and less convinced that the action of the District was going to stop Donovan. The police investigated their complaints carefully, because this was not the first time that they had heard allegations of Donovan's sexually assaultive behavior. Unfortunately, when they brought the cases to the district attorney, they found that in Stone's case, the statute of limitations for filing formal charges had run out. The district attorney was still unwilling to file Simpson's case because of "insufficient evidence."

The press report that the charges had been dropped was taken by many members of the congregation as vindication for Pete Donovan. In fact, all it revealed was that the district attorney was not willing to risk filing a charge against a well-known and well-regarded community figure based only on the report of a woman, with no other witnesses to what occurred. The fact that complaints of criminal conduct were brought and investigated should, in and of themselves, have alerted the membership to the seriousness of this situation. But the lingering unspoken assumption that women frequently cry "rape" falsely in order to get men in trouble prevented many from comprehending the significance of this piece of information.

On August 30, Maxwell Kelley sent a letter to all the clergy and local church presidents in the District, outlining what had transpired in Donovan's case. Kelley felt compelled to get some information directly to the other churches because of the publicity the preceding week. This letter, however, did not go to members of First Church. In his letter, Kelley acknowledged the need for an open disclosure:

The women involved are hurt and angry. They and we have been advised by experts that for therapeutic reasons this whole situation should be aired. We must confess that though we spent much time discussing how to make it widely known with all parties concerned, satisfactory solutions could not be found. The story was leaked to the press (not by us) and what followed is history. The wounds are now exposed and the task of healing has only begun. We are in close touch with the women, and their welfare is very much our concern. But the members of First Church also need our love and understanding. The members are confused and hurt. . . . The officers have been torn between their need to protect their minister, the good name of the church, and yet deal with the issue of justice for those who brought the charges. . . . This church is a broken body. It will need all the support and love and wisdom that we can offer. . . .

Kelley's letter continued by noting that an interim minister had already been called to serve First Church during its search for a new pastor. Finally, he specifically acknowledged that the District found its procedures for discipline of clergy inadequate and that it would be revising these procedures immediately. In his cursory summary of the events of the previous months that led up to Donovan's resignation of standing, Kelley acknowledged the victims; but he still did not indicate the nature of the charges which were brought against Donovan. He seemed more comfortable to let the newspapers take care of that.

Following his abrupt departure from First Church, Pete Donovan requested another meeting with the ministry committee. Somewhat reluctantly, the committee agreed to meet with him even though their process had been concluded with his resignation. Donovan proceeded to present his own defense. He had brought along supporters to confirm his version of the facts. He asserted contradictions in dates, places, and individuals. The core of his presentation was his belief that he was the victim of conspiracy. Finally, the committee realized that Donovan was engaging them in a hearing—that is, a hearing of his defense. Once again he was in control. The committee chairperson then stopped the process and reminded Donovan that he had foregone a hearing and the opportunity to present his defense when he voluntarily resigned his standing. The committee was not willing to listen further to his presentation. Donovan retorted, "I resigned because I knew I would not get a fair hearing and because then all of these lies would be public information and this would ruin me." Finally, the committee, realizing how Donovan was still manipulating them, concluded the meeting by reassuring him: "If you want a hearing, you can have one. All you need to do is ask for it and the files will be opened." The meeting adjourned and Donovan left quickly.

On September 4, Ralph Bennett again met with the women victims. He told them that three more women had come forward. Once again they pressed: When will an official letter go to the members of First Church? Bennett could not make any promises at this point. They needed this letter now more than ever; it was now their only hope of vindication.

The next day Bennett met with Don Ivy, the president, other First Church officers, and one of the most recent victims to come forward. They agreed that a letter should go out from the District and local church officers. How and when was unclear.

On September 7, the First Church newsletter appeared. An article summarized the open meeting that had taken place on August 28. Still there was no mention of the nature of the charges or of the need to support the women who had brought them. The article did note, however, that contrary to the impression left by some of the news articles, Donovan would not be "permanently barred from the ministry. The only restriction is in this denomination." Once again the women felt discounted.

Three days later, Don Ivy met with the women to inform them that, as a result of the recent meeting with yet another victim, the locks on the church would be changed in order to deny Donovan access to the building. The women reacted to this news with mixed feelings. It was a concrete act by First Church leadership to prevent Donovan from continuing to use the church. Why had it taken one more victim to get some movement from the officers? Still they pressed Ivy. He dodged their plea for assurance that a congregational letter would in fact go out.

On September 11, Rev. Katie Simpson decided that she would communicate directly with the other clergy and local church presidents in the District. She began her letter to them with a summary of charges that had come from the women's testimony to the ministry committee: that Donovan had engaged in sexual contact (including intercourse) with counselees and employees; manipulation, coercion, and intimidation of parishioners; and forced sexual intercourse. Her discussion of the subsequent events emphasized the lack of response from First Church and the District during the two years between 1982 and 1984. She concluded,

Of the many issues that remain unresolved, the women ask;

1. Will clergy sexual misconduct occur again in our church, our District, or our denomination?
2. If it happens again will a woman be willing to initiate grievance procedures realizing she faces disbelief, ridicule, and months, possibly years, of inaction?
3. What process would be effective and efficient to deal with violations of ethics?

Let us work together to guarantee justice, insure safety, and encourage spiritual growth by resolving ethical issues directly and professionally as the lay and ministrial leaders of our community.

Although some of the missing pieces of the story had now been given to the wider church, they were still not available to First Church.

On September 20, nearly one month after Donovan resigned, the officers finally sent a letter to the membership of First Church. Summarizing again the meeting on August 28, they reassured the members that Dr. Donovan had been fairly dealt with according to the procedures of the District and that his resignation was of his choosing. The letter included one significant paragraph:

There is one matter which continues to slow the healing process. The women who brought charges against Pete Donovan have been portrayed by some as "gossips" and "flakes." Those women who are members of this church, and some of the people who have given them support have felt ostracized by other members of the congregation. We would plead for an understanding that the charges, which were varied in nature, were presented with seriousness and at great personal cost to the women. Their action in bringing their allegations to the District Minister and to the Ministry Committee was appropriate and necessary. The safety and well being of the membership of the church and the integrity of the church in the community was in question.

This was the first time the powers-that-be acknowledged publicly the price the women paid to try to repair the church's integrity. It had been a long time coming.

The officers' letter concluded with the assertion that the "exact nature of the charges" would remain private, but the offer was made to discuss the "nature of the charges" with any individual or group in the church. The officers remained convincingly obtuse. The initiative lay with the members to seek it out. Only one person came to Ivy to ask for more information, and even then Ivy felt bound to discuss the charges only in generalities.

Ten days later, most members of First Church received a lengthy letter from Bernie Mitchell, one of the six women who brought charges. She provided the background and some particulars that had been missing. She told her story as a victim of Donovan's misconduct and explained the actions the women had taken:

Dear friends:

Although there have been meetings and a recent letter sent out by the church officers, there still seems to be some confusion regarding the circumstances that led to Dr. Donovan's resignation. As one of the women involved in bringing charges, I thought it might be helpful to present a chronological account of what led up to the decision to file charges with the District. I am sending this letter to a few people I feel might be willing to pass the information on to others, and to others that I have known for a long time and have worked with on various projects. I would prefer, of course, to contact each of you personally, but this would take more time than I have available.

I have been attending the First Church of Newburg for over 50 years, beginning way back when my mother first brought me to Sunday School in the downtown church. (I am sure she is probably turning over in her grave at all the recent events that have beset a church she loved very much.) I mention this for the benefit of the newcomers to our church and to give some credibility to my concern for the well-being of First Church. Also I wish to state that I am writing this letter on my own initiative and mailing it at my own expense.

Because of the confusion surrounding Dr. Donovan's departure, some who have been associated with our church for a short while are disillusioned, disbelieving, and/or angry. Others, who have attended for many years, share these feelings and are considering joining other churches. Many feel that Pete was an excellent preacher and very helpful in times of crisis. No one can question that Pete is a dynamic, charismatic man and a good public speaker, and I am sure he did help a lot of people—*but this was his job.* This is what a minister is expected to do and *paid* to do. What a minister is *not* expected to do and is not paid to do is to harm people and to take advantage of counseling situations where people are very vulnerable. (Any *reputable* person in the "helping" professions—ministers, attorneys, psychiatrists, etc.—is very careful not to become personally involved with those who come for help in times of need.) Likewise, an accountant who is hired to keep track of the financial records of a business may be a very good accountant, but if funds are also being misused at the same time, sooner or later he/she will be in trouble.

During the past 4½ years of Pete's tenure with us, many will say that attendance has skyrocketed. However, if one looks at the church attendance record (which is kept faithfully each Sunday), it will show that although attendance increased dramatically during the first year (which would be expected), it leveled off during the second year and has steadily decreased since that time. Although many new people joined the church, an ever-increasing number left. The early morning service at the Enchanted World tourist attraction was never a success. I was very involved in the set-up and beginning of this program and I can state categorically that very few people from the area attended the services. Although a few families joined our church, and have become active members, by and large, the majority of attendees at the early service consisted of people from First Church who came to the early service to support Pete, and the attendance figures recorded each Sunday in the book mentioned above include the program participants, the ushers and greeters, the technical staff, etc., as well as those who attended the service. I personally made this count each Sunday and was told to include *everyone.*

At that time, I really believed that Dr. Donovan was seriously dedicated to the growth and well-being of our church and the people. As was true of many others, as a member of his staff, I was caught up in his charisma and grandiose ideas, and I went along with many activities that I *knew* were questionable, but I also had a great need to be needed and Pete is an expert in recognizing the needs of people and using them to promote his own interests. Even when I finally realized that Pete's plans and programs were not in the best interests of our church, at least from my viewpoint, it took me six months to get up enough courage to resign as a member of his staff, so I am well aware of how difficult it must be for many of the church members and friends to accept all the recent publicity concerning the charges that were brought by the six women that eventually led to his resignation.

Mitchell provided a chronological summary of the events leading up to Donovan's resignation and then continued,

Prior to this sequence of events, none of us knew each other very well. However, as time went by, calls were received from other women with similar complaints, and we were appalled by the growing evidence that something was very wrong concerning Pete's behavior, especially as a minister. We decided to investigate what could be done to bring this to the attention of the church leadership and the District for some action. In the process, we found that Pete had left his former parish for similar reasons, and later, the church he served before that one confirmed that he left there for the same type of misconduct.

As our investigation continued, we found that other women in the community (outside our church) had brought complaints of sexual abuse involving Dr. Donovan to the Women's Advisory Council, a group concerned with problems encountered by women in the county. Since this Council reports to the County Council, eventually the matter of Dr. Donovan's behavior became a "community" problem as well as a "church only" problem. Although there has been concern about the publicity in the media, it is very difficult to keep this kind of information "private" when it is brought to the attention of community leaders. As far as I know, personally, the "leak" to the press did not come from either our group or from the District.

When the group of women from the church filed charges with the District, we did so because we were convinced that this was the only way to stop Dr. Donovan from continuing his unprofessional behavior in our church and in the community. Jesus said in Luke 17:3, "If thy brother trespass against thee, rebuke him, and if he repents, forgive him." This seemed to apply to this situation. After several meetings with the District staff people a meeting was arranged with members of the Ministry Committee (as detailed in the recent letter you received from the church officers). Each of us appeared privately before that committee and told our story. When that committee agreed that the charges were serious enough to warrant a hearing, we each prepared and signed a statement of our individual charges and were fully prepared to face an ecclesiastical hearing with Dr. Donovan. We understood that our charges would be presented to Dr. Donovan and that he had the option of facing the charges and clearing his name or voluntarily resigning with charges pending. Since he *chose* to resign, the statements were sealed and will remain so until and unless he subsequently attempts to seek employment as a minister in our denomination.

I would like to mention that one of the conditions for our agreeing to have our statements presented to Dr. Donovan and to face a hearing was that the District immediately would send a letter to the members of First Church, explaining the process and stating the nature of the charges. This letter was never sent. While it was Dr. Donovan's prerogative to choose to resign with charges pending, the women were disappointed that the hearing did not occur. It would have been painful, but at least the matter would have been out in the open. As it is, many people are confused about what really happened – and this confusion has been exacerbated by Dr. Donovan's negative derogatory comments regarding some of the women involved in the charges, despite the fact that part of *his* agreement with the district was that he would not harass us in any way.

Some of you who receive this letter may still think that Pete Donovan walks on water and will not believe a word I have said. This is a risk I am taking. It does pain me, however, that a number of people that I have known for many years, have worked with, have considered to be my friends, have chosen to blame the women for "chasing after Pete," or have lightly dismissed the whole issue with remarks like "boys will be boys," despite the overwhelming evidence that Dr. Donovan was asked to leave at least two (and possibly five) churches for similar incidents of sexual misconduct. On the other hand, I understand Pete's tremendous power of persuasion and intimidation – and probably we all must share some of the guilt for letting this kind of situation persist for so long a period of time.

It is my hope that those who care about our church will not leave because of what has happened. Dr. Donovan's credentials, presented to the Pulpit Committee who brought him to Newburg, were impeccable, and if the Presidents and the District were slow to respond to the complaints, we need to be forgiving and understanding, because a lot of people, both women *and* men, regardless of age and experience, were taken in by his manipulative tactics. He has had many years of experience in this area, and we are, for the most part, mere novices. Keep in mind that at least two, and possibly more, former churches chose to let Dr. Donovan leave and gave him glowing recommendations. It took great courage on the part of the women who brought charges, our church officers, and the District to finally challenge his behavior.

What we need now, it seems to me, is for those who care about the church to help with the healing process. While we need to move on, it may be necessary to attempt to answer questions for those who still feel angry, disillusioned, and betrayed. We can't simply sweep the whole thing under the rug—but we can choose to love each other, even though we may never agree on all aspects of how this situation was handled. If you feel you were helped by Pete, this should not be discounted. At the same time, I feel that there is overwhelming evidence to support that many people were hurt during his ministry and this cannot be ignored either. Those of us who brought charges felt that it was imperative that our church and our District should not allow Dr. Donovan to leave without giving him the opportunity to respond to the charges brought against him.

I feel also that we need to forgive Dr. Donovan, forgive the church Presidents, forgive the District, and forgive each other—and then go to work to help our associate minister and the new interim minister to build up the Church School, the Youth Group, and to provide programs and activities that will be inspiring and uplifting. Those who are coming back to church need to see friendly, familiar faces; those who are angry need our love; and those of us who brought the charges need your understanding (we really feel very isolated), and the church needs your help and support, now more than ever before.

I hope the above will be helpful and answer some questions for those who have been confused about the sequence of events leading to Pete's resignation. You may feel free to pass the information on to others who also may have questions. . . .

Mitchell closed by inviting anyone who wished to gather at her home to ask questions and discuss all that had occurred. Twenty-five people attended. They were glad finally to have some information. Their reaction was, "How come we were not told about this?" As active members of the church, they felt that they had been deprived of information they needed. They were right.

Mitchell's letter was the most caring pastoral act that had occurred in this congregation in the past three years. She was determined that the whole church should have the information it needed in order to deal with its pain. Although she hedged on the embarrassing and painful details, including her own, she did not gloss over the injustices. But she also moved beyond them to anticipate healing and reconciliation for the church. Mitchell loved the church too much to allow it to go on hiding its head in the sand and suffering from its own fear and avoidance. She could easily have given up hope for the church at any number of points, but she did not. In this final step, she exemplified what the church can be: a community of faith which can face itself, call one another to account, and be reconciled through a just response. Her action, far more than that of any of the designated leadership, finally made this a possibility.

Lina Robinson was very concerned about the toll all of this took on Bernie Mitchell. She believed that Mitchell should not have had to bear the weight of providing public disclosure to the congregation. Some of those who did not attend the meeting blamed Mitchell for all the uproar because she talked about it openly. Others blamed the women who had made the complaints for all the disruption in their church. When Donovan left, they felt the loss of the hug or the pat they ordinarily got from him on Sunday morning. If they did not have any other intimacy in their lives, this weekly touch by a charming man seemed to fill a need. They were angry when it was taken from them. They did not want to believe the allegations.

Many, however, knew that something had been going on; they just did not know what. After the first shock wore off, many of the long-standing members did believe the allegations. The fact that the television news reported the story held great credence for many of them. Lina Robinson asserted that the local church leadership had hedged too much about informing church members. She said she almost wished at one point that the denomination had a bishop who would come to them and say what was what and what would be done about it. Initially, people were trying to be "charitable," which meant that they were worried about what was being done to this poor clergyman. But many members simply hungered for information that could help them understand their experience and put it in perspective. Without this information, closure still eluded the congregation.

A year later, in 1985, it seemed from the outside that the congregation was in relatively good shape. Financially, First Church did not suffer when Donovan resigned, even though many of Donovan's strongest supporters left with him. A number of people who had not been coming to church returned. They liked the new minister. Robinson felt that once the dust settled, First Church was really stronger than before Donovan came.

But even then, Donovan's presence overshadowed the congregation. Selected First Church members received an invitation to Pete Donovan's wedding. The bride was to be a nineteen-year-old woman who had previously been a member of First Church's youth group. Donovan had dated her when he first came to First Church and she was fifteen years old.

5. How Could This Happen Here?

The major difficulty for many members of First Church in believing the information they were hearing about their pastor, Peter Donovan, was a belief that such things do not really happen; and if they do, not in their church. What did occur is unbelievable, but true. How could a credentialed, highly regarded, well-liked pastor in a mainline, middle-class Protestant church do such things and get away with it for so long? How could someone like Donovan operate unimpeded within the church? How could an institution like the church take more than three years to deal with the allegations of abuse that were presented to it? How could all of these things happen at First Church in Newburg?[1]

Three primary factors created an environment in which Peter Donovan was able to offend relatively unhindered in First Church. These factors leave other churches unprotected from pastoral offenders. First, the church is myopic about the problem of abuse by clergy. Although the problem has existed for years, the church remains unprepared to address it. Second, the power of the pastoral role is a power seldom acknowledged, particularly in denominations with a strong congregational polity. Third, the familial model of congregational life is assumed at First Church as it is in many churches. When the family serves as the model for interaction, then incest is a possibility within the church family just as it is within other families. These three aspects, common to church life, made it possible for a pastor who was a sex offender to carry out his activities with little fear of ever being caught.

The Church's Myopia

The first precondition for pastoral abuse to occur was the myopia of the institutional church.[2] Not having anticipated such a situation, the church did not have adequate policies and procedures with which to process these particular complaints of unethical conduct. No reference was made to such things in the constitution of First Church. The only general reference in the District's bylaws related to "conduct unbecoming a minister." Rarely if ever had it been necessary to apply this provision to the discipline of a clergyperson.[3] There was no definition of "unethical behavior" or "conduct unbecoming a minister." There was no process specifically to adjudicate a complaint of unethical conduct. There was no delineation of disciplinary options should the complaint be well-founded.

The lack of policies that specifically addressed sexual misconduct of clergy in the professional role was not accidental. For both liberal and conservative churches, there is a vacuum in addressing clergy ethics. Neither is prepared to deal with the problem, but for different reasons.

Conservative churches deny the existence of the problem as long as possible. When they cannot deny it any longer, they deal with it as a matter of the pastor's adultery, ignoring the issue of professional ethics.[4] Since many conservative congregations are independent or minimally affiliated, there is no denominational structure to monitor or discipline clergy. Thus the weight of any response often rests alone with the local church. The matter may or may not be addressed.

For liberal churches, a different vacuum exists. The District to which First Church of Newburg belonged illustrates this well. The District had gone to great lengths in the past few years to remove any reference to clergy sexual conduct from any policies under which it operated. In the past, rules addressing sexual conduct of clergy had been used primarily to deny ordination and employment to qualified lesbian and gay pastors. Removal of such references was an attempt to protect the privacy of all pastors with regard to their personal lives. However, these well-motivated actions, which sought not to prescribe sexual behavior for clergy's private lives, left the District with no standards of *professional* conduct. Consequently, it had no policy to deal with abuse and unethical behavior in the professional, pastoral role. Here a misapplication of the scriptural instruction to "judge not that you not be judged" left the church with no means to judge unethical professional behavior that harmed parishioners and the church.

Both the conservative and liberal views summarized here are confused as to the nature of the problem. Both see the problem as one of *sexual* deviation: For the conservative, the deviation is from the strict norm of monogamous, heterosexual marriage, and thus they condemn it as adultery; for the liberal, the deviation is also from a norm of clearly defined sexual conduct, but they overlook it as a "private matter." Neither is able or willing to view the matter of sexual contact by clergy in a professional, pastoral relationship as a professional issue of misuse of power and authority which is by its very nature abusive and exploitive. When the problem is viewed as an issue of pastoral abuse of power, it is the right and responsibility of the church to prescribe professional behavior, limiting the pastor *in a professional role* from engaging in sexual activity with those whom he or she serves.

The Power of the Pastor

The desire for peer relationships between clergy and laity is common where the church is seeking to overcome the ravages of years of authoritarian clerical leadership. However, this desire fails to acknowledge the very real difference in power between a pastor in a professional role and those whom he or she serves. Social ethicist Karen Lebacqz comments:

The fact that professional power is legitimated and institutionalized has tended to blind us to the importance of the mere existence of that power. Precisely because it is legitimate power—authority—we forget that there is a significant power gap between professional and client. We also forget that it is a type of power that is very difficult for clients to overcome.

The vulnerability of client to professional differs from the vulnerability of friend to friend: the professional can not only hurt my feelings, but has legitimated, institutionalized power to make significant changes in my life.[5]

The power and authority of the pastor come from training, credentials, and gifts as well as from the contract given by the laity to the pastor.[6] The pastor's role and responsibility require a degree of intimacy with church members, but this intimacy is imposed and not reciprocal.[7] Because of this, the power dynamics between the pastor and the laity are always unequal.

In such a setting, to say, Trust me, I'm a professional, is to enhance the power gap. The notion that professionals are trustworthy *reinforces* the power gap, though it is intended to make professionals accountable. The image of the professional as altruistic and not interested in self-gain works to undermine any suspicion the client might have about the amount or type of power that professionals attain. . . . Indeed, we want professionals to have power: power to heal, power to litigate, power to set things right with God or nature or other human beings. We purposefully give professionals legitimated power: authority. But with it comes the power to define our needs and problems as well as respond to them. And with the power of definition comes a significant control over our lives. We want them to use it for our own good.[8]

In addition to the power and authority given a pastor as a professional, the symbolic power of the pastor as religious leader magnifies the professional role. "The minister is a physical representation of the whole community of faith, of the tradition, of a way of viewing the meaning of life, . . . and of God."[9] The importance of this dimension should never be underestimated.

A healthy professional, pastoral relationship realizes the fact of pastoral power, acknowledging both the gift that it brings and the implication that the pastor is at risk to misuse that power. The laity are vulnerable to harm should that occur. The risk of misusing the power is a risk for all pastors. This risk is a function of the role itself, not just of the character of the pastor. Since we can no longer assume that a pastor by definition is altruistic, trustworthy, and virtually accountable to no one, steps must be taken both by clergy and laity to prevent the misuse of this power. Only then can we maintain the integrity of the pastoral relationship.

A Paradigm of Family

The church is frequently referred to as the family of God. Jesus referred to his followers as his siblings and to God as his parent. This image suggests the positive parallels of trust, intimacy, caring, commitment, and respect, which should be the bases of human family life. Within the church, there are particular roles and responsibilities related to divisions of task and authority. These roles determine expectations of pastor and laity. The pastor's role is clearly defined in terms of responsibility to provide for the needs of the congregation; this role carries with it the assumption of trustworthiness. Clergy, whether they like it or not, are in a role of authority in relation to the laity, just as the parent is in a role of authority in relation to the child. This is not to suggest that clergy are to play a parental figure to the childlike laity, but rather to acknowledge that the clergy-lay relationship in the church is not a peer relationship.[10] Either role of parent or pastor can be misused. Like a parent with children, the pastor may experience sexual attraction to members of the congregation or to counselees, or may be approached by a member who is attracted to him or her. The responsible pastor does not respond to these attractions by engaging in sexual activity with the parishioner, but instead seeks to guide and direct with the best interest of the parishioner in mind. When the irresponsible pastor does engage in sexual activity with parishioners, the result is incest in the church family; the parallels to incestuous abuse are disturbing.

When Rev. Dr. Pete Donovan came to First Church, he was trusted unconditionally. This was the way one related to one's pastor, with the same trust one had in one's parents. Just as a father has access to his children, Donovan had access to the women of First Church. As their pastor, he had the prerogative to initiate contact with them; he had reason for regular visitations to conduct church business or to attend to their pastoral needs.

Because of his role and their expectations, they did not use the same good judgment about him as they would have used with someone else. None of the women would have become involved with Pete Donovan had he not been their pastor. Their guard was down and he used that to his advantage.

Each of the First Church members whom Donovan victimized was taken in by what they thought to be his warmth and caring, both emotionally and sexually. They liked being "special" in his eyes. The women who initially acquiesced to Donovan's sexual approach questioned the wisdom of their relationships with Donovan once they learned that they were not the only "special" one. But as long as the secrets were kept and they believed they were his only intimate relationship, they were able to disregard their ambivalence and hesitation. They were isolated, confused, and self-blaming; they did not seek help from the outside for fear of not being believed. They saw clearly that the rest of the church regarded Donovan highly; who would believe such a story?

Donovan expected the victims to protect him by keeping the secret. The secrecy not only promoted an illusion about the victims' relationships with Donovan, it also allowed Donovan to function without challenge. The First Church family was by and large unaware of his activities; thus any rumors about Donovan being a womanizer were casually put aside. Those who did have information but chose not to act on it out of fear or loyalty colluded in the family secret. Donovan's ability to enforce the secrecy was finally overcome by the sheer numbers of women with whom he was involved.[11] As one of the victims observed, "How could he have assumed that we would not find each other? Most of us have been in this community for years and we talk to each other; women talk to each other about their experiences." He was counting on each woman's silence to protect him; he was not worried, because he never expected anyone to talk.

When the women did speak out, they were often not believed, especially by other members of First Church. Prompted by Donovan, the First Church family closed ranks behind their pastor and collectively vilified the six women, preferring to "save the family" rather than protect the women. The women had revealed the family secret and they were punished for it by being cast out of the church family. Fortunately, none of the women who initially came forward recanted. Although they often felt lonely, isolated, and fatigued by their efforts to get someone to do something about this situation, they did not succumb to the pressure they felt from First Church to deny their experience of abuse by Peter Donovan. If they had, he would still be there and would still be causing harm to members of First Church.

Predictably, Donovan denied the allegations and sought to discredit the women who brought complaints. He explained their motives in terms of congregational politics and their desire to "get him." Although he acknowledged his sexual activity with some, he denied the coercion and force they alleged. He asserted that women were always after him. In his denial of responsibility, Donovan essentially "blamed the victims."[12] Finally, he explained to the press that when you were a widely known public figure, you had to expect this kind of thing occasionally. The father figure rallied the church family in order to maintain its image of him and of itself. The facade began to give way only when denominational officials intervened from the outside. Yet through the months of turmoil, the family myth remained: These things cannot happen here.

The adoption of the familial mode of church life in recent years is well motivated. Using this model, the church has sought to build relationships among members of genuine love and care, providing in some cases a family for those who have no families. However, the implications of the readily accepted model have been largely unexamined. For example, the model raises unrealistic expectations of emotional intimacy for its members. It requires time and energy that would be better used in establishing and nurturing family relationships and friendships. It usually follows a patriarchal model of family, with male roles limited to decision making and control and female roles limited to nurture and childcare. It can sustain the secret of incest to the detriment of its members.

An alternative model for healthy congregational life would be that of community as distinct from family. Community life is also based on values of respect, mutuality, compassion, and care, but with a lesser degree of intimacy. Using this model, the expectations for emotional or sexual intimacy would be lessened and the opportunity to question authority or unethical behavior of church leaders would be more readily available.

A Pound of Prevention

Perhaps "How could this happen here?" is a moot question. A more relevant question might be, "Why hadn't it happened before?" The answer for First Church is simply one of luck. They had not crossed the path of an offender before. The right conditions were all in place, as they are in most churches. The point is that every church is vulnerable to the pastor who is unethical or who is unconcerned about professional boundaries in pastoral relationships. Given this fact, we must give more attention to prevention.

Prevention for the individual pastor begins in seminary training. Seminarians, as well as ministers already serving, deserve information and clarification of ethical standards for ministry. They also deserve a challenge to their naiveté about the role of pastor. They need to understand the nature of the power and authority of their role and the responsibility that goes with it. They need to learn how to maintain boundaries in relationships with parishioners and counselees. They need to learn to care for their own emotional and sexual needs in appropriate ways. They need to be encouraged to seek consultation with professional peers in order to avoid isolation in their pastoral roles. These aspects of preparation for ministry will help caution "wanderers" from wandering and will help the otherwise conscientious pastor avoid mistakes which can destroy his or her ministry.

Prevention for the church should focus on unequivocal policies and procedural safeguards to help churches avoid hiring an offending pastor. However, since even these preliminary provisions cannot guarantee avoidance, education of the laity and clear policies and procedures can encourage early disclosure and intervention to stop an offender.[13]

The most important step that the church or any institution can take to prevent a reoccurence of the events at First Church is to discuss openly the problem of the pastor's violation of professional ethics. Until this all-too-common problem is brought into the light of day in the church, the experience of the First Church of Newburg will be repeated over and over. Countless people will be harmed and will leave the church. Lawsuits will proliferate. The profession of the ministry will continue to lose its credibility until it becomes one of the least-respected professions in our society. These are the tragic consequences of the unethical behavior of the few.

Although this issue has existed for years, the church has refused to see and refused to prepare itself to deal with it. The structure of the church aided Donovan, albeit unwittingly, never confronting his behavior, passing him along to the next church, and finally hesitating in the face of abundant evidence of his betrayal. It is small wonder that this time the church did act. The fundamental ideology and structure of our religious institutions must be examined and changed if we are to minimize this occasion of sin.

6. Doing Justice and Mercy

And Jesus told them a parable, to the effect that they ought always to pray and not lose heart. He said, "In a certain city there was a judge who neither feared God nor regarded the people; and there was a widow in that city who kept coming to him and saying, 'Vindicate me against my adversary.' For a while he refused; but afterward he said to himself, 'Though I neither fear God nor regard the people, yet because this widow bothers me, I will vindicate her, or she will wear me out by her continual coming.' And the Lord said, "Hear what the unrighteous judge says. And will not God vindicate the elect, who cry to God day and night? Will God delay long over them? I tell you God will vindicate them speedily. Nevertheless, when the Child of Humanity comes, will that one find faith on earth?"

LUKE 18:1–8

Nevertheless, we must also face the fact that there may be times when the individual may be served with less than justice in order to satisfy the needs of the community.

WILLARD GAYLIN, *The Killing of Bonnie Garland*

Dr. Peter Donovan's betrayal of his pastoral role was a clear case of injustice. Among those who had full information, there was never any question about the truth of the allegations of his unethical behavior. The pattern and consistency of his behavior with each of the six victims who came forward, as well as with others, was more than convincing. Although the formal allegations of misconduct were never adjudicated, there is no doubt the ministry committee would have concluded from a hearing that Donovan was guilty of "conduct unbecoming the ministry." Did the Reverend Dr. Peter Donovan cause harm to innumerable people? Did he cause harm to First Church? Did he undermine the credibility of the profession of the ministry? The answer is a threefold yes.[1]

Justice and mercy are the only means we have to repair the consequences of injustice. In the context of a religious community, these should be the first items on a pastoral agenda and the focus of the church's response to complaints of this nature. Justice and mercy are not abstract ideals to be discussed at arms' length, but are the very essence of what is needed to heal the brokenness caused by injustice. If we begin with clarity about the specific consequences of specific injustices, we can address the individual needs of those harmed. Then we can seek to do justice and mercy in concrete and substantive acts and thereby create a glimmer of possibility of healing and reconciliation.

The Consequences of Injustice

The harmful consequences of Donovan's injustice were many: Some were experienced by all the victims, others were a function of their individual life circumstances. Psychologically, sexual interaction with their pastor destroyed the women's sense of trust and safety. They were flattered initially by his attention and their self-esteem was enhanced momentarily, but they soon felt ashamed and guilty.[2] With hindsight, they struggled with their naiveté and their decisions to get involved with him.

Marian Murray and Bernie Mitchell felt stupid to have been duped by Donovan. They saw themselves as mature women who should have known better than to be taken in by a smooth-talking younger man. Joan Preston was incredulous that she allowed the promise of marriage to suspend her better judgment. Nancy Linder's self-esteem, already minimized by abuse, eroded even further. These four women felt betrayed, exploited, and victimized when they realized that they were not "special" and the "one and only."[3]

Kristine Stone and Katie Simpson felt betrayed, exploited, and victimized by being forced into sex they did not want. This betrayal was especially difficult for Kristin Stone, due to her youth and generally trusting nature. Her grief over the loss of idealism and trust in people was very painful. Katie Simpson had to face the fact of her vulnerability when confronted with Pete Donovan's male aggression. All the women were depressed and anxious[4] about disclosing their experiences and the impact this would have on their families. They were also worried about trying to stop Pete Donovan.

In addition, whatever issues existed before for the women who had sought counsel from Donovan remained among their immediate needs. Nancy Linder was confused and left alone to deal with her abuse. Marian Murray's son was still in crisis. Kristin Stone was still grieving the loss of her teacher. They felt disappointment that this pastor, whom they expected to help deal with their problems, not only failed in that but also caused them more problems.

Once they recognized what had been done to them, it did not take long for these women to get angry. Yet even in the midst of their anger, they all felt fear because Donovan had verbally threatened them and they believed that he could be violent. The resulting stress and anxiety caused exhaustion, sleeplessness, and other physical difficulties.[5] For Bernie Mitchell, the long months of the intervention process and subsequent events seemed to sap her strength and finally to reactivate her cancer. Too weak to fight any longer, Mitchell died in the spring of 1986.

Donovan's unethical behavior also damaged the women spiritually. As their pastor, Donovan had access to the women's deepest and truest selves. The women looked to him not only as counselor, but as spiritual guide and protector. The psychological pain he caused was magnified and took on cosmic proportions. Not only were the women betrayed by a trusted professional, but they were betrayed by one who professed to represent God: Hence they felt betrayed by God as well.

The women's confusion and ambivalence was countered by Donovan's theological and moral justifications: "The person to whom I look for guidance in matters of faith and practice is engaging me in activity which I thought was sinful and yet he says it is God's will that we should love one another."[6] The victims who had betrayed a monogamous commitment to a partner bore additional layers of guilt and confusion. Donovan reassured them that there was nothing wrong with their genuine love for each other.

The stakes were high. Because the women felt betrayed by the one who represented God to them, and in that betrayal felt betrayed by God, the foundations of their relationships with God were shaken. Because the church did not act adequately in response to their call for help, they reasonably concluded that neither God nor the body of Christ was present to them in their suffering. This crisis became a crisis of faith. Seeing the church as a source of pain, suffering, deceit, and betrayal, the women initially withdrew from involvements with First Church. But fortunately for the wider church, they refused to withdraw completely. Like the persistent widow, they kept coming back, demanding that it do something about Donovan.

In the aftermath, they each evaluated their church involvement. Kristin Stone continued to teach Sunday school, but she was unsure if she would remain; she considered joining another church. Joan Preston was vehement: "This has been my church for over twenty years; I'm not going to leave because this man is tearing it apart. Staying away isn't going to make it better; if all the women who were hurt stay away, it just allows him to separate us from the church." Preston continued to serve on the mission board. Bernie Mitchell tried to relate to First Church until her death, but the ostracism she experienced wore her down. Rev. Katie Simpson refused to allow Donovan to limit her ministry, but she has had no further contact with First Church. Nancy Linder and Marian Murray completely severed their ties with the church.

There is no way to measure the damage done to the lives of these six victims. There is no way to know how many other victims have also carried the burden of violation by Peter Donovan. Donovan's pattern of abuse began shortly after his arrival at First Church in the spring of 1980. During the next year, Donovan abused and assaulted four known victims, then another in early 1982, and another in early 1984. Did Donovan victimize others during the intervening months? Did the confrontations by each of the women and by several of the First Church and District leaders during those four years have a chilling effect on Donovan's behavior? Were there periods when he was not offending? It is difficult to know, because there are victims who have not and will not come forward. Clearly, however, the investigation and process that led to his resignation did not discourage him. The last known victim to come forward was approached by him during August 1984, while the ministry committee was investigating him.

Donovan's ultimate victim was First Church itself. The psychological and spiritual price was high here as well. Old friendships forged over time through common interest and work in the church were lost. Those who had some information about the seriousness of Donovan's behavior were discounted by friends who refused to believe them or support their efforts to deal with Donovan. Trust was destroyed. These relationships remain sundered, and, in the opinion of some, can never be healed. The congregation of First Church was nearly destroyed. Even though Donovan backed off from his empty threat to withdraw the church from the denomination, he still succeeded in breaking it apart. Nearly a hundred members left when he did. Many of these supported him and left because they were offended by the way he was treated. But others left because they were offended by the church's ineptitude in dealing with his offenses. In any case, Donovan created a place of fear and distrust, pitted people against each other, and left broken bodies and spirits in his wake.

An Ethical Framework

Seeing the consequences of injustice does not always lead us to remedy them. Thus the question is, why should we respond to injustice? When should we be moved to redress unjust balances of power or to heal unjust injuries? We are called by a moral imperative to do justice and mercy, an imperative that rests on three fundamental assumptions. First, people can and should *act* in the face of injustice rather than remain passive and uninvolved.[7] Second, embodiment is a crucial fact of existence which requires that we take violations of bodily integrity seriously.[8] Third, relationship between and among people is a primary value.[9] Two additional principles gleaned from feminist and liberation theologies give direction to this ethical framework: We must begin with the lived experience of people, and take the side of the powerless and victimized. Together these assumptions and principles mandate a response to the consequences of injustice.[10]

Without realizing it, the six women who came forward with complaints about Peter Donovan's treatment of them were using this ethical framework to respond to this injustice. First of all, they acted, individually and collectively, rather than remaining passive. Each of them believed that something had to be done. Second, they knew that Donovan's deceit and assaults were fundamental bodily violations and not to be disregarded. Third, they placed high value on relationship. Thus when Donovan initiated a relationship with each of them, they assumed that it was genuine. Even in the face of Donovan's betrayal, they each returned to confront him and to try to get him to seek help.[11] Their relationships to their church were of such importance that, rather than walk away, they worked within the system to bring necessary changes. Finally, they pleaded with the church to take their experiences seriously and to stand with them in their powerlessness and victimization. Motivated by their faith and their intuitive sense of ethics, they did what they could to stop the injustice of Peter Donovan so that others would not be hurt. What they expected and deserved from their church was justice and mercy.

Doing Justice and Mercy

Micah's admonition (6:8) to do justice and mercy and to walk quietly with God most clearly summarizes the church's responsibility to its people in this instance. Justice-making is central to the teachings of both the Hebrew and Christian scriptures and to the doctrines of the church. Yet the expectation of justice is seldom applied to circumstances of interpersonal relationship, and even less often applied to the workings of the church itself. In the situation Peter Donovan created, profound injustice occurred in both areas. Brokenness abounded. Doing justice in this situation was the only viable means to restore right-relation.[12] Seeking mercy required support for those broken by Donovan, binding up their wounds and attending to their needs. In this case, both were less than adequately fulfilled.

What are the particulars of doing justice? What does it look like when we do attempt to restore right-relation? What are the specific acts of mercy? Truth-telling, acknowledgment of the violation, compassion, protection of the vulnerable, accountability, restitution, and vindication are the requirements for doing justice and mercy in the face of violation and injustice. (Justice and mercy are discussed here as ethical norms and expectations, not legal ones. In a purely legal arena, the concepts are very different and may not serve to restore right-relationship.) It may be helpful not only to describe these requirements, but also to reflect on their implications in this particular case.

Truth-telling

Truth-telling in these kinds of situations happens when the silence surrounding the secret of abuse is broken. Truth-telling is not merely a rendering of the facts; it is giving voice to a reality. When victims can give voice to their specific experiences of violation, the secret loses its potency. These victims finally felt safe enough to come forward and tell their stories to each other and to the church. But the victims were nonetheless at great risk, and required protection from Donovan's intimidation. The fact that there were six of them strengthened their resolve. During the negotiations with Donovan, when the women lost their right to speak publicly, the secret of the abuse regained its power and stifled the healing of First Church.

Acknowledging the Violation

But for justice to be awakened and informed by truth-telling, the truth told of violation must also be truth heard. The church to whom the truth is spoken must be able to hear and believe in order to act. In hearing the truth, the church *acknowledges the violation* that has occurred. This acknowledgment was never forthcoming for the women in this instance. Albert Bandura observes that "justified maltreatment can have more devastating human consequences than acknowledged cruelty."[13] The absence of acknowledging the cruelty of injustice serves to justify the maltreatment. Thus we should never underestimate the power of the explicit acknowledgment of violation in the process of healing for victims. Simple though it is, verbal acknowledgment conveys a depth of understanding and compassion that cannot be accomplished in any other way. In this case, some individuals by their actions and responses clearly believed the women. But no one, on behalf of the church, said, "You have been harmed by the actions of this pastor. This is wrong and should never have happened. We regret that it happened to you."

Official acknowledgment can be communicated by a procedure that is put into play immediately upon receipt of information that harm has been done. Appropriate procedures clearly convey to the victims that the church is taking the situation seriously. Adjudication of the allegations through this process can provide vindication for the victims, the broadest possible acknowledgment of their experience.[14] The consistent efforts by First Church and District leaders to circumvent the process and avoid a hearing, combined with the years it took to get any action, did little to instill confidence in the women that the church was hearing their truth and acknowledging their violation.

Compassion

Compassion is the willingness to "suffer with" another person coupled with the desire to alleviate the suffering. Often in our own discomfort at another's circumstances, we try to minimize, explain away, or avoid her suffering. We may tell ourselves that it is out of our concern for her pain that we do these things but, in fact, it comes from our discomfort. We simply want to avoid sharing another's suffering. We wish the problem would go away. Compassion is the willingness to be present, acknowledging and listening, even when we cannot solve the problem. Very few people were willing to suffer with Peter Donovan's victims.

Protecting the Vulnerable

Protecting the vulnerable from further abuse is a work of justice and mercy. Once we are aware of the potential for abuse, it is incumbent upon us to do all that we can to prevent further harm. When we knowingly allow harm to continue, we are colluding in it. In this case, protection would have been partially accomplished by suspending Peter Donovan from his pastoral duties for the duration of the process.[15] His suspension would have minimized his access to additional victims in the church and gained the additional benefit of stifling his attempts to rally support and split the church. Ralph Bennett tried to protect the victims by warning Donovan that he should not attempt to have contact with the women, but this did not seem to prevent his trying to intimidate them.

Accountability

Accountability is the focus of Jesus' teaching in Luke 17:1–4: "If your brother sins, rebuke him, and if he repents, forgive him . . ." The church has the prerogative to expect its ministers to be accountable. Accountability begins with confrontation and expects repentance. Although Donovan was confronted by all six of the women and by at least four church leaders, he was never officially confronted, held accountable, and faced with the consequences of his actions. He never confessed and never accepted responsibility for the harm that he did. He skillfully prevented such a confrontation by avoiding a hearing. He lost his job and his standing as a minister in one denomination, but his reputation was essentially intact. Having painted himself as the innocent victim, he was free to continue his manipulation and deception in the community. The consequences to him were minimal.

Negative consequences may be punitive, but they may be the most direct route to true repentance. Donovan was never given the opportunity to repent, that is, to turn from his transgressions and "get a new heart and a new spirit" (Ezekiel 18:30–31), to acknowledge his acts and take responsibility for them. He deserved that opportunity. Willard Gaylin argues that "those of us who transgress have a right to *receive* punishment; if we are not punished adequately for our crimes, we are being treated as less than persons. . . . As a tribute and testament to [the agressor's] freedom, we must dignify him by making him pay for the evil actions he commits. We show our respect by making him accountable."[16]

Restitution

Restitution, making payment for damages, is a concrete means of renewing right-relation. Not only does material restitution help pay for the actual expenses often incurred by victims (for example, the cost of therapy), it also carries a symbolic meaning. It is a tangible effort to restore that which was lost when the offenses occurred. Because Donovan was never held accountable, there was never any possibility of his making restitution to the victims. This was one of the reasons that the women considered bringing a civil suit against Donovan. They hoped that it would offer a concrete symbol of their vindication and restoration. They also hoped that requiring Donovan to pay damages might convince him that he could not afford to continue his harmful behavior. Although restitution is usually made in financial payment for injury suffered, it can also refer to less tangible forms of restoration. For example, if Donovan had acknowledged the harm that he did and taken responsibility for it, this would have restored the victims' reputations in the community and could have inspired genuine sympathy for them from church members. This could have brought about renewal of right-relation between the victims and church members.

Vindication

Ultimately, *vindication* for the victims is the substance of justice and mercy. Vindication refers not to vengeance and retaliation, but to the exoneration and justification of those who have experienced harm, made legitimate complaints, and consequently been imputed. The obsolete definition of vindication is "to set free." Surely the physical, emotional, and spiritual key to healing from violation is to be set free from the multiple layers of suffering it created. This is the promise given by Jesus in the parable of the persistent widow: "And will not God vindicate the elect, who cry to God day and night?"

Approximate Justice

Perfect justice in response to the circumstances discussed here would have required that each of these aspects of justice be pursued. The church's response would have been immediate, the process open and equitable. As a result, the victims would have been vindicated; Donovan would have acknowledged responsibility, made restitution to the victims and to First Church, and taken steps to repent. The members of First Church would have been fully informed of the events and their resolution. Then healing of the wounds and fractured relationships could have begun and forgiveness and reconciliation would have been possible.

It would be nothing less than understatement to say that it is rare for the church (or any institution) to bring forth perfect justice in the face of injustice. This is a fact of contemporary institutional life. Even for an institution that purports to believe in the values that underpin justice, doing justice – especially within the institution – is an ideal, seldom achieved. But somehow we still expect that an institution like the church will be true to its own calling, rise above the ponderous inadequacies of its worldy institutional incarnation, and do what is absolutely right. It will not. It may do the best it knows. It may bring forth approximate justice.

Approximate justice is a difficult reality to accept. This is especially true in a time when so much that surrounds us is corrupt and oppressive, diminishing the person on all sides. We long for a place where justice will confront corruption and oppression, where, even if we cannot prevent these sins, at least we can call them by name. In the whole of our lives we long for a place of peace and serenity, of safety and protection. So, regardless of theological persuasion, we come to the church seeking something other-than-worldly, something true and good. When we do not find perfection there, we create it in fantasies. One fantasy says that bad things do not happen in church; everyone is happy, just, and good. When bad things do happen here, we are unwilling to give up our fantasy and so we are prone to deny the truth and deny the truth-tellers. In so doing, we multiply the injustice. The other fantasy is that when bad things do happen, the church, unlike other institutions, will act with swift and sure resolve to correct the harm done. When it does not, we feel betrayed and angry, and can become cynical.

In the face of harm perpetrated by a representative of the church, it is incumbent upon the church to do its best to do the works of justice and mercy, that is, to approximate them. In the process of addressing the injustice done, it should seek to do least harm.[17] Approximate justice is a realistic expectation to have of the church. It is the best means we have available to heal the wounds deeply. Victims deserve more, but should at least receive approximate justice.

In the face of harm perpetrated by Peter Donovan, the church at some points acomplished approximate justice and at others fell short of it. Unfortunately, its shortcomings outweighed its accomplishments. Some of the victims came forward at great risk and the truth was told little by little. But First Church was not prepared to hear it. The leaders did not press for the specifics they felt they needed to act decisively. The wider church hesitated for months before it finally began to act. There was never unqualified official acknowledgment of the victims' suffering, and expressions of compassion were few and far between. Some efforts were made to protect the women from Donovan's intimidation. But other women were not protected, because Donovan was not suspended. The final step of removing Donovan from First Church and denying him the option to practice ministry in the denomination was accomplished. But Donovan was not held accountable, experienced few negative consequences, and controlled the process to the end. The victims did not receive restitution and were hardly vindicated by his departure. They are still vilified, ostracized, and misunderstood by the vast majority of members of First Church, most of whom still do not know what Donovan did.

As I pondered my own ambivalence at being thankful for the approximate justice that was done and being angry at what was not done, I realized that I was almost willing to accept that approximate justice is all we can expect from the church. I was willing to accept that it is a waste of energy to work for more than that. I was almost ready to advocate for approximate justice as the goal toward which we should strive, simply because more did not seem possible. But then I confronted the question that would not leave me: Why was it impossible for these women to get perfect justice from the church? At least three dynamics seem to mitigate perfect justice and leave us with approximate justice in this situation: "shooting the messenger," misnaming the problem, and "blaming the victim." Each of these is an automatic, institutional response to the revelation of internal injustice. But each of these obstacles to justice reflects the patriarchal nature (that is, the historical and contemporary domination by men) of the institution: This is the key to answering our question. I finally realized that women will never find perfect justice in a patriarchal institution. We can only expect approximate justice, not because people are incapable of something more, but because patriarchy will not allow anything more.

"Shooting the Messenger"

Pastors' unethical behavior is not a new phenomenon; nor is it a new phenomenon that women who come forward to complain about such things are discounted and scorned. In 1872, Victoria Woodhull published the revelation that Henry Ward Beecher had long been sexually involved with a parishioner, Elizabeth Tilton. Woodhull was subsequently jailed on the charge of "passing obscenity through the mails," but was later acquitted.[18]

"Shooting the messenger" is a common response to the revelation of unethical conduct. When the news is not something the institution or the community wants to hear, its knee-jerk reaction is to turn on the bearer of the news, often with a vengeance. First the messenger's credibility becomes the issue, and then her or his motivation is suspect. All of this serves to deflect the attention of the church from the real source of the problem, the unethical pastor, and it relieves the church from doing anything about it. This phenomenon was particularly evident in the response of First Church to the complaints being made public in the media. The congregation directed its anger and hurt against the women and Rev. Ralph Bennett. They turned on the victims and their supporters with an irrational desire to drive them from the church in order to preserve their illusions about Peter Donovan.

Misnaming the Problem

Institutions also avoid doing justice by misnaming the problem. Whenever the issue of clergy sexual contact with parishioners arises, the most frequent concern of clergy is to express their need to be protected from seductive, manipulative parishioners. Their anxieties surface immediately and they name the problem of clergy-parishioner sexual contact solely in terms of *their* "vulnerability to seduction."[19] This concern comes from clergy's very real anxiety about interacting with parishioners; it is best described as the pastor being "at risk" in ministry. The risks are many. They include the sexual approach of a parishioner, false accusations of misconduct, or misusing pastoral power only to meet the pastor's needs. But although the pastor is *at risk*, it is only the parishioner who is *vulnerable*. Parishioners look to a pastor to meet their needs for guidance, counsel, support, and care. In seeking help from someone who is a designated authority, who offers to provide these services, and who holds power, parishioners are vulnerable and thus able to be harmed or taken advantage of.

The difference between the pastor's risk and the parishioner's vulnerability is a qualitative reflection of the difference in power. The pastor has the power and the responsibility to maintain the boundaries of relationships with parishioners.[20] Thus the problem of clergy-parishioner sexual contact is not the fact that the clergyperson may at times feel attraction to a parishioner, nor is it the sexual initiative of a parishioner (although this can certainly be problematic). The problem is the pastor who acts on his or her feelings of attraction to a parishioner, or the pastor who responds affirmatively to a sexual initiative from a parishioner. This pastor crosses over boundaries intended to protect the pastoral relationship. A clear understanding of the nature of this problem may allow both church bureaucrats and members to confront an alleged offender more quickly, rather than to seek so readily to protect him.

"Blaming the Victim"

"Blaming the victim" also stifles doing justice. Social scientist Albert Bandura observes that:

When bad practices are well entrenched, efforts on the part of concerned individuals to halt them by publicizing their destructive effects are more likely to arouse derogation than sympathy for the victims. To acknowledge the inhumanities arouses self-critical reactions if one does nothing about the situation. It is easier to reduce the discomfort by designating the victims as a bad person than to challenge bad practices that are an accepted part of the social order.[21]

This was certainly the case at First Church. In effect, those who tried to stop Donovan by telling of their experiences with him were rocking the boat and were asking the leadership to do something the leadership felt powerless to do. They instead sought to reduce their discomfort by blaming the victims: "Donovan was young and attractive and women were always after him"; "I don't see how a strong woman like her couldn't resist masculine hands"; "Those women were consenting adults and they knew what they were doing." It is an interesting paradox that blaming the victim inadvertently admits the truth of the allegations. It simply seeks to turn responsibility for the events back on the victim. In this case, attention was deflected away from Donovan as the cause of the problem; his practices had become "an accepted part of the social order."

The Power of the Patriarchy

These impediments to doing justice are bound to occur in a patriarchal institution such as the church. An examination of this structural issue is critical if we are to prevent future occurrences. As Lebacqz comments,

The question is not simply whether the individual practitioner abuses the individual client. The question is also whether the social construction of reality provided by the profession is one that adequately reflects the needs and interests of society, or whether it perpetuates biases and unjust structures.[22]

In considering this question as it applies to the church, we would have to conclude that the church does not adequately reflect the needs and interests of society, certainly of women in society; and that it does perpetuate biases and unjust structures, particularly with regard to women.[23] Questions of women's ordination, women's employment as pastors, contraception, inclusive language, abortion, sexuality, and so forth continue to be major unresolved issues in our churches. The structural power of the churches is still dominated by men, while the grassroots population is mostly women. As a result, women's experience is still rarely considered in theology, ethics, doctrine, or pastoral care. If considered at all, women's experience carries an overlay of the image of woman as temptress, source of evil, and "gateway to hell," as Tertullian wrote. Thus it is no surprise that a local church structure dominated by laymen selected Donovan and, when presented with allegations of his conduct against women, could not or would not take the women's experience seriously enough to act immediately to stop him.

Some churches today echo the theology and practice Matilda Joselyn Gage critiqued in 1893:

The fact that ministers of the reformed church were permitted marriage did not change priestly teaching that woman was created solely for man, and they found apologies in the Bible for illicit conduct. These Protestant clergymen taught, as had the Catholic, that a priest was incapable of sinning; and from the Sermon on the Mount, "To the pure all things are pure," was quoted in proof of this assertion. Even when under circumstances of great personal peril and danger to life, the trust of parishioners in the morality of their shepherds was often abused; of this, Rev. David

Williamson, one of the most eminent Presbyterian ministers of Edinburgh, was a conspicuous example. In defense of his immorality Mr. Williamson said, "Verily, I do not deny that with St. Paul I have a law in my members warring against the law of my mind, and bringing me into captivity unto the love of sin which is in my members.". . . The excuse they [the ministers] made . . . was "where sin abounds the Grace of God super abounds; there is no condemnation in those that are in Christ."[24]

Although I do not propose to ascribe this grievous situation simply to sexism, we must realize how the patriarchal structure gave license to a man like Peter Donovan to use his pastoral role and position in the church to engage in the abuse of women for years and then protected him from the consequences. Needless to say, if Donovan had been engaging in the same conduct with men that he did with women in the church, he would have been relieved of his pastoral privilege long ago. But the fact that the victims were women, the acceptance of the adage that "boys will be boys," and the hesitancy of some men to confront other men's behavior all meant that the women had to look initially outside of the church for a sympathetic ear and a person willing to act. The patriarchy prevented the women from getting justice within the church.

Too Many Lessons

There are many explanations for the shortcomings described here, but there are no excuses. Ignorance and its close companion, fear, shaped the responses of many people. Donovan used fear tactics to try to control the primary players. He threatened to withdraw First Church from the District. District leaders never called his bluff. He explicitly threatened First Church leaders with lawsuits and damage to their public reputations should they attempt to act. He thought he could control them and expected them to "handle the situation" for him. They refused to be his pawns, but they were unwilling or unable to challenge him. Whether out of ignorance or fear, the passivity of the designated leaders of First Church in response to the women's revelations was, at best, inadequate.

Ultimately, withholding information from First Church members was the most unfortunate decision made in the process. The leaders in good faith believed they were acting to protect the church. Yet tragically, this provision of the agreement has done the most to prevent healing in the congregation. It was the most painful betrayal felt by the women. It was received with deep ambivalence by First Church members: They asked, "Why weren't we told?" and said, "We don't want to know" in the same breath. Some of the First Church leaders who were involved still feel it would have been a mistake to have revealed the specifics of the charges to the membership: "There was no reason to do it; nothing would have been gained by airing our dirty linen." Other leaders finally conceded that sharing that information would have put a stop to the rumors, clarified the seriousness of the situation, and possibly engendered sympathy for the victims.

With the advantage of hindsight, as we look with a critical eye at the events set in motion at First Church by Dr. Pete Donovan, we can speculate about the turning points and learn some concrete lessons. What if the District minister or members in Donovan's previous church had conveyed the actual reason for his leaving that church? What if the search committee at First Church had followed up on the vague references and their own nagging discomfort that something was not quite right? What if First Church had had a specific reference in its contract with their pastor listing the professional ethical standards they expected to be upheld? What if the two presidents of First Church, rather than just feeling hamstrung by insufficient information from the victims, had solicited the additional information they needed? What if the District had responded immediately to the complaints by utilizing the formal procedures for adjudication and discipline? What if Donovan had been immediately suspended and the congregation informed of the proceedings? What if, in the face of Donovan's intransigence, the District had gone ahead with the hearing and not given away its opportunity and responsibility to inform First Church? What if, at the open meeting at First Church after the resignation was tendered, I had delineated the charges the women had made so that the congregation would know?

Associate District minister Rev. Ralph Bennett and the women who brought complaints had been concerned all along about the gaps in the process and the general hesitation among many to deal with the problem of unethical pastoral behavior. Once they had done all they could to stop Donovan, they turned their attention to an evaluation of the policy and procedures that had been used. They changed and refined the existing process based on what they had experienced in this case. They then went beyond that to press the national denomination for action. They wanted other districts and local churches to benefit from their experience rather than having to learn the hard way.

The policies and procedures had to be rewritten in order to provide for:

• suspension of pastoral duties as soon as formal, written complaints are made against a pastor
• use of the process for confrontation and adjudication rather than attempting to circumvent it "pastorally"
• notification of the local church members of the nature of charges and the process to be used to adjudicate them
• a hearing required rather than used as leverage for achieving voluntary resignation
• the hearing structured to provide the opportunity for fair treatment of the accused *and* of the victims
• the clout of the denomination (local and district levels) brought to bear without hesitation or apology in disciplining the offending minister
• information about offending pastors' offenses passed along when references are requested

The bottom line of the recommendations is a clear recognition that the church is responsible for the professional conduct of its clergy and must act to prevent misconduct from causing harm to its members or the community at large.

The lessons learned over those last months were numerous and painful. For First Church members, the pain of disappointment was still very immediate. Lina Robinson observed somewhat pensively: "At first, I was angry at all that he did. Then I was angry at myself for not having been able to do more to stop it. But now it's just sad. So much potential gone wrong. It's a real shame. I guess we'll just go on. But we can't just go on. He's still here."

For the women victims, their trust in the church was tested and shaken. They believed that the church would do what was right when faced with the facts. Their naiveté buoyed them for a while, and then their anger sustained them through the ordeal. Like the persistent widow, they realized that *they* had become regarded as the thorn in the side of the institution. They also realized that any semblance of justice they might receive was unlikely to be for the right reason, but would rather be (to paraphrase Luke), "because they bother me, I will vindicate them, or they will wear me out with their continual coming."

Months after Donovan left First Church, Marian Murray wrote to me:

"I've thought about returning to church and have decided that the whole experience was such a negative one for me that I don't want to be reminded of it or be a part of an institution that refused to accept responsibility for the safety of its membership. If the local leaders had chosen to deal with it in a straightforward manner and suspended him until it was resolved, I would have been more satisfied. Allowing him to remain in the pulpit through that summer while we met with the Ministry Committee and then allowing him to determine the conditions of his departure did not indicate to me that they took our concerns very seriously. That local leadership has never recognized that the women did indeed make a valuable contribution to the integrity of the church. We are comfortable with the action we took but I occasionally wonder what more we could have done to bring about a more satisfactory resolution."

Surely, they did all that they could. Sadly, it was not enough. And even more sadly, no one ever thanked them for what they did. This was one of the most painful realizations for the women. Not only were they ostracized and defamed by many First Church members, they never received any appreciation for the fact that they had been willing to risk their privacy and their safety as well as spend a great deal of time and energy in order that injustice be stopped and justice and healing begin. The church never realized nor acknowledged the gift bestowed by these women. They were faithful to the church even when it was unfaithful to them. Such faith is a rarity and a blessing.

Interestingly, no one ever urged the victims to forgive Donovan. I was struck by the absence of this phenomenon because it is usually the first response many people make to others' victimization. There may be two reasons for this conspicuous absence. First of all, some people simply did not believe the women; they would have had to acknowledge the truth of the women's experiences in order to encourage them to forgive Donovan for his misconduct. Second, those who did believe the women may have sensed that the shortfall of justice was such as to preclude the possibility of forgiveness by the victims.[25] Bernie Mitchell urged forgiveness in her letter to the congregation because for her, the acts of justice had been sufficient to allow her to take the step that *she* needed in order to let go and move beyond the pain she had experienced. But she could not and did not speak for the rest of the victims.

Even though no one urged the victims to forgive Donovan, many have urged them to forget. In 1987, three full years after Pete Donovan left First Church, a long-time member of the church stopped by to see Marian Murray about some city business. As their visit drew to a close, she asked Murray why she had not returned to First Church. As they talked, Murray realized that her visitor knew very little about the charges against Donovan and did not know that she, Murray, had been involved. Murray filled in the picture, explaining that she was the first victim to come forward. The member consoled Murray with the suggestion that since this was all in the past, Murray should return to church. Although well intended, this advice betrays the most fundamental lack of understanding of what the women lived through. It is the very thing that Jeremiah warned against, seeking to "heal the wound lightly." As Willard Gaylin observes, "Time does not heal all wounds, and the amount of time needed to heal the majority of serious wounds is well beyond that which the unwounded could ever anticipate."[26] Instead of forgetting, the women still need to hear acknowledgment and appreciation from members of First Church.

Perhaps the hardest lesson for all of us who were involved was that in the face of injustice and the harm that resulted, the best we could achieve was some small measure of approximate justice. The women and the church deserved more, but more was not possible. Yet in spite of the institutional myopia and inertia, due to the efforts of many people, at least a measure of approximate justice was accomplished. It is never enough, but it is all we have while we strive for more. The question is, in this case, was the justice sufficient to make possible some healing for those most deeply wounded?

Epilogue

The subject of the so-called philandering clergyman has fascinated authors and readers for years. From Hawthorne's classic morality tale *The Scarlet Letter*, to John Updike's insipidly sympathetic *A Month of Sundays*, to John D. MacDonald's critically insightful *One More Sunday*, the combination of so-called illicit sex and the pastoral persona has held a special intrigue. It has also carried an aura of unreality. The common perception is that these things, like soap operas, do not really happen: Ministers are not really sexual with their parishioners. For the most part, this is true. Most pastors do not misuse their pastoral office the way that the Reverend Dr. Peter Donovan did. Most pastors maintain the sacred trust bestowed upon them when they are ordained. But some do not. And those who do not, few though they may be, seriously diminish the credibility of the majority who do.

Webster defines *charisma* as "an extaordinary power (as of healing) given a Christian by the Holy Spirit for the good of the church." Charisma is a gift given by God for a specific purpose. It has always been acknowledged in the life of the church with thanksgiving and celebration. Saints recognized and unrecognized have been gifted with charsima and used it to provide leadership and witness within the church: Saint Joan of Arc, Saint Catherine of Sienna, Martin Luther King, Jr., Anne Hutchinson, Pope John XXIII, Howard Thurmann, and many others remain as memorable figures in church history. The gifts of teaching, preaching, prophecy, healing, and administration have built up and sustained both the institutional church and the faith community.

But Webster's second definition of *charisma* is equally important: "a personal magic of leadership arousing special popular loyalty or enthusiasm for a public figure." Some might say that this is the secular equivalent of the Christian definition; but, in fact, it is the opposite of the previous definition. It is a gift from God gone awry. Its purpose is to build and sustain the adoration of a public figure, not to enhance the well-being of a body of people. It elicits unconditional positive regard and uncritical loyalty from eager followers. Unfortunately, people are attracted to both kinds of charisma. Discerning the difference can be difficult. Charisma is paradoxical by its very nature.

This is the tragic paradox of Peter Donovan. He is undeniably an extremely gifted person. He is attractive, stimulating, and engaging. His gifts of preaching, personal interaction, and administration are well-suited to the needs of the church. But these gifts have been put in the service of the manipulation, deception, and control of others. Somehow the potential to do great good has been skewed and distorted and the result is great evil. No sin is greater than the misuse of that which was created for good. Nowhere is this more painfully evident than in the misuse of sexuality. Peter Donovan's sexual abuse of women in the church was a profound distortion of sexuality and the pastoral relationship. His charisma run amok made it possible and sustained his self-deception. As one member remarked, "Pete thought he had done nothing wrong. To him, every action he has taken has been above and beyond the call of duty. He believes that he is right." It is doubtful that he will ever acknowledge what he has done and that it was wrong.

The tragedy of Donovan, like Henry Ward Beecher before him, is best described in this editorial written in 1868 by Theodore Tilton, lecturer, publisher, friend of Beecher, and husband of Beecher's lover:

When a man of unusually fine organization, with high-strung nerves, with a supersensitive conscience, with a tremendous sensibility to reputation, and with a boundless ambition, suddenly, by one act, sacrifices the slow honors of a lifetime, there is something in his self-destruction to excite the pity of mankind . . .

To such a man the agony is that there is no restoration. The crime leaves an ineffacable stain. He looks back upon a violated ideal. He can never again be his former self. . . . He may become in many respects a wiser, nobler, cleaner man—taught by experience and chastened by suffering; but nothing can prevent the remainder of his life from being, to his own thought, a vanity. Whoever else may pardon him, he cannot pardon himself. Every day's sunshine will mock him, and make him see the shadow of his soul. No bird will ever sing in his ear without reviving his innocence as a memory and his guilt as a fact. He is like one who has lived his appointed span. The grave awaits him. Death is his next friend.

A man with a sword in his soul, giving him a wound that never heals, exciting in him an agony that never sleeps, filling him with a despair that never takes a ray of hope—if any human creature deserves sympathy, this is the man.[1]

There is so much at stake and so much is lost when a person of extraordinary gifts takes the path of arrogant disregard and deception, not by one act, but by many. Even in the face of a pattern of misconduct, some still respond with sympathy. But others respond with grief, anger, and contempt.

It will be difficult for the church to protect itself from the misuse of charisma. It could overreact in the face of events like those told here and deny the presentation of gifts, assuming that they always portend evil. Or it could regard the circumstances presented here as a tragic but extraordinary event in the life of the church and ignore the lessons contained herein. Its longing for the gifts of charisma would thus overrule its good sense.

For the church, the gifts of charisma must always be regarded critically. They must be constantly tested in light of the well-being of the faithful community. When they are not functioning "for the good of the church," they must be turned away. Just as any relationship or attraction to another should be tested at regular intervals in terms of the health and well-being it promotes, so must the church maintain a critical edge in relation to its charismatic leaders. Blind, unthinking, unconditional loyalty to anyone is the basis of tyranny and injustice. It is no less so in the church than in secular society.

What happened at First Church of Newburg could happen in any church or any institution. I chose to write about First Church not to open old wounds, although they need opening and cleansing, and not to confront Peter Donovan, although he needs confronting, but to vindicate all of the women who were harmed by him, and to prevent future harm. In telling their story, I have tried to distill the lessons the church and other institutions must learn if we are to sustain the sacred trust of our professional relationships.

Appendix:
Sexual Misconduct by Clergy
within Pastoral Relationships

This is a working document developed by the Northwest District of the American Lutheran Church in 1987. It is offered as a model of a procedure which can be adapted to other denominational structures providing a response to complaints of unethical professional behavior by clergy. The story told here was in no way connected to the development of this particular document. For more information, contact: The Center for the Prevention of Sexual and Domestic Violence, 1914 N. 34th St. #105, Seattle, WA 98103. (206) 634-1903.

Preface

"Simon, son of John do you love me . . . ?
"Feed my lambs." "Tend my sheep." "Feed my sheep."

To be a pastor is to be entrusted with a sacred responsibility, "to care for the church of God which was obtained with the blood of his own Son." Not only is the pastoral office a position of great trust and responsibility, it is also, by virtue of the trust persons place in the office and the person of pastor, a position of great authority and power over others.

It is unthinkable that anyone would violate that trust and power for the sake of personal gratification, and yet the experience of the church is that it does happen. Persons in pastoral roles may betray the trust placed in them by misusing power in many ways. These guidelines deal with the specific abuse of power by those who engage in sexual advances toward or contact with those for whose spiritual welfare the pastor is responsible. Any improper or unwanted sexual contact is damaging. The harm is increased many times when the contact comes from a person to whom the victim has every right to look for guidance, protection, and care.

When persons are injured by the actions of its servants and representatives, the church itself and its message are also compromised.

These guidelines are intended to help the church deal sensitively and responsibly with such violations of the pastoral office. In itself such action is a part of the pastoral responsibility of the church which, in the policy of the Evangelical Lutheran Church in America, is entrusted to synodical bishops. As in all pastoral actions, sin and injustice are to be dealt with in the light of God's word and with a view to the well-being of persons, the honor and integrity of the church and its pastoral office, and the credibility of the gospel.

The church in dealing pastorally with offenses and offenders must not only adhere to accepted legal standards of justice and due process, it must also be guided by the law and the gospel of God and by the Spirit of God who alone knows how and when to apply both law and gospel in exercising the church's authority to bind and to loose, to forgive or not to forgive sins.

Forgiveness and restoration to positions of trust for persons who have violated that trust should not be quickly or lightly given. "Do not be hasty in the laying on of hands, nor participate in another person's sins; keep yourself pure," (I Tim. 5:22). At the same time the goal should always be to restore even the most serious offender to fellowship with God and communion with the church, even when forgiveness and reconciliation cannot be extended to include restoration to public office. "Brothers and sisters, if anyone is overtaken in any trespass, you who are spiritual should restore that one in a spirit of gentleness. Look to yourself, lest you too be tempted." None of us is safe from temptation. Certainly the temptation to sexual impropriety is inherent in our own sexual needs. The very loving intimacy involved in good pastoral care can provide the occasion for offense unless the pastor is spiritually and emotionally alert and watchful. The prevention of sexual abuse by pastors is also a concern of the church. These guidelines are intended to help the church, its people, and pastors deal in healthy ways with the pastor's sexual nature and the demands of the pastoral office so that persons in need of counsel and support can continue to come to their pastors with confidence and trust.

Assumptions Underlying This Policy

Pastors or pastoral counselors are *always* responsible for the emotional, spiritual, and physical protection of persons who come to them for help or over whom they have *any* kind of authority. Breach of this protective relationship is improper and/or unethical.

Persons accused of sexual misconduct are to be considered innocent until the accusation has been substantiated beyond a reasonable doubt.

The protection of those involved including the victim or victims, the accused and the accused's family, the congregation or institution shall be maintained until all facts have been carefully considered and appropriate actions determined.

Because pastors/pastoral counselors often deal with individuals who are emotionally and psychologically fragile or personally vulnerable it is imperative that a) the pastor/counselor himself or herself be healthy psychologically, emotionally, and spiritually, and b) that he or she have adequate preparation and education for helping those individuals under their care and have continued supervision to deal with the inherent risks caused by dependency and/or transference.

Sexual contact between a pastor and a parishioner, client, or employee with whom the pastor has a professional, pastoral relationship is unethical and unprofessional behavior and shall be deemed as sexual misconduct. Sexual misconduct is defined as sexual activity or contact (not limited to sexual intercourse) in which the pastor or pastoral counselor takes advantage of the vulnerability of the parishioner, client, or employee by causing or allowing the parishioner, client, or employee to engage in sexual behavior with the pastor or pastoral counselor within the professional relationship. Such behavior is "conduct incompatible with the character of the ministerial office" (see ELCA constitution 19.15.01. Footnote E5).

This policy applies to pastors in the Evangelical Lutheran Church in America. The term 'pastor' in this document shall apply to pastors or associates in ministry who serve in a professional or voluntary position of pastoral responsibility (involving personal contact and care for others) in a congregation or church related agency.

The term church, as used in this policy, refers to the Evangelical Lutheran Church in America, its whole and its parts; i.e., synods, congregations, ministry. When referring to the local parish served by a pastor the term congregation will be used.

Policy for Dealing with an Alleged Occurrence of Sexual Misconduct

Any complaint or allegation of sexual misconduct (as defined in this policy) shall be brought to the immediate attention of the synodical bishop (or his/her representative). If circumstances warrant, the bishop may immediately suspend the accused pastor temporarily from his/her pastoral duties with the congregation or agency he/she serves (with pay and without prejudice); in this event, the bishop shall notify the congregation or agency of the investigation and insure that the congregation has adequate pastoral services during the period.

When a complaint or allegation of sexual misconduct is brought to the attention of the bishop the bishop shall ask the Synod council or its executive committee to select members from the consultation committee to form the special consultation committee which shall meet with the person(s) bringing the complaint forthwith in order to:

A1. hear her/his allegations directly,
A2. request that complainant(s) prepare a written complaint,
A3. request permission from complainant(s) to use the written complaint and her/his name in discussion with the accused pastor,
A4. attempt to secure the complainant(s)' willingness, if requested, to appear before the committee on discipline for a formal hearing,
A5. outline the process which will be followed in response to the complaint.

Once the written complaint is received and if the special consultation committee believes that there is sufficient cause for concern that there may have been some violation of professional ethics, the special consultation committee shall meet with the accused pastor in order to:

B1. present him/her with the formal, written complaint,
B2. outline the process which will be followed in response to the complaint; emphasizing the presumption of innocence and the right to due process,
B3. hear his/her response to the complaint directly (may be verbal and/or written),
B4. make available a summary of the pastor's response to the complainant for comment.

If there is sufficient cause for concern that there may have been some violation of professional ethics, the special consultation committee shall proceed.

The special consultation committee shall presume the innocence of the accused pastor until unethical conduct is proven.

The special consultation committee shall not ask the complainant and the accused pastor to meet together during this phase of the process.

If not already accomplished, in order to protect the rights of the accused pastor and to protect the complainant(s) and congregation from possible harm during the investigation:

C1. the special consultation committee shall recommend to the bishop a temporary suspension of the pastor from pastoral duties, with pay and without prejudice,

C2. the bishop shall notify the congregation or agency of the investigation, temporarily suspend the accused pastor, and appoint another pastor to serve temporarily. The temporary pastor shall be fully informed of the circumstances of the temporary suspension in order to minister effectively with the congregation.

The special consultation committee shall fully investigate the accusation through information and documentation from the complainant, the accused pastor, and other credible sources as appear appropriate.

Based on the investigation carried out by the special consultation committee, it shall, using its best judgment, determine the veracity of the complaint and recommend action to the Bishop as follows:

D1. IF THE ALLEGATIONS ARE NOT SUBSTANTIATED by the special consultation committee, the investigation will cease and every effort will be made to exonerate the pastor. A record of the process and its conclusion will be provided for the pastor and may be included in his/her personnel file. A public statement of exoneration by the bishop may be made if the pastor so chooses. The bishop and special consultation committee shall respond with care and concern to the complainant(s) and to the congregation or agency as appropriate.

D2. IF THE ALLEGATIONS ARE SUBSTANTIATED by the special consultation committee and the offense and consequences of misconduct are determined to be relatively MINOR, the special consultation committee will recommend that the bishop shall take the following steps:

• issue an *educative advisory* in response to a situation which is not necessarily unethical but shows poor professional judgment. He/she should provide clear guidance in order to accomplish the necessary corrective.

- issue an *educative warning* in response to a situation of unquestionably inappropriate and unwise behavior but which is not clearly unethical. It is expected that this clear warning will bring a cessation of the behavior.

- issue a *reprimand* in response to a situation which involves unethical behavior but which resulted in relatively minor consequences. This action will be recorded and placed in the pastor's file.

The bishop, using his/her best judgment and in light of the recommendation of the special consultation committee, will determine what action to take and will meet with the complainant, the accused pastor, and representatives of the congregation or agency (separately) to communicate and explain the action taken. This action will be communicated in writing to all parties as well.

D3. IF THE ALLEGATIONS ARE SUBSTANTIATED by the special consultation committee and the consequences of the misconduct are determined to be relatively MAJOR, the bishop shall recommend that the committee on discipline hear the case. The committee on discipline shall proceed with a hearing to determine its action in this matter utilizing the section on Consultation, Discipline, Appeals, and Adjudication ELCA Constitution and Bylaws, (Section 19.15.01–05).

If the committee on discipline finds the accused engaged in unethical behavior, they shall take one of the following steps:

- *Censure* the pastor in response to clearly unethical behavior which was persistent and resulted in (or could have resulted in) serious harm to others. This action shall be recorded and placed in the pastor's personnel file but may not result in suspension. Restitution and rehabilitation may be recommended.

- *Suspend the pastor temporarily* from the clergy roster in response to unethical conduct which resulted in harm to others and to the ministry. Protection of others from further harm is paramount. The suspension shall continue until there is clear evidence of rehabilitation and restoration of the pastor (see below "Response to Offending Pastor"). At that time, the pastor may petition the committee on discipline which originally reviewed the case (or if unavailable as many of those originally hearing the case as possible with new members coming from the appropriately elected synodical or church committees on discipline) for cessation of the suspension.

• *Suspend the pastor permanently* from the clergy roster in response to unethical conduct which resulted in substantial harm to others, the church, and the ministry and, in the face of which, there is little possibility of rehabilitation and restoration to ministry. Protection of others from harm and protection of the integrity of the ministry are paramount.

Any of these actions shall be recorded and placed in the pastor's permanent personnel file.

D4. APPEAL PROCESS: The appeal process shall be followed as outlined in the ELCA Constitution and Bylaws (see Footnote 5).

Once the committee on discipline has made its determination and taken a disciplinary position, the following steps should be utilized.

Responses to the offending pastor:

Confronting an offending pastor with the disciplinary action of the bishop and/or committee on discipline should be understood as a pastoral and caring act of the church. It provides the greatest potential for both vocational and personal redemption and healing.

For personal healing confession and absolution are the gifts of God to bring the reality of forgiveness for even the most grievous offense. Those ministering to an offending pastor must remind the offender and be reminded themselves of the depth of God's grace and the cost of God's forgiveness in Christ.

Rituals of confession and absolution are meaningful ways to convey the word of God's grace in the midst of the enduring human realities of guilt, repentance, remorse, and discipline. Rituals of confession and absolution, while given freely and gladly, should be practiced with care and not in haste.

While confession and/or acknowledgment of responsibility for misconduct shall be regarded as an important first step in the possible restoration of an offending pastor to effective ministry, it is important to distinguish between confession and absolution, on the one hand, and restoration to pastoral ministry, on the other. The nature of pastoral authority combined with the intimate access of the pastor to vulnerable people facing emotional struggles, such as loss, disablement, and divorce, requires a high level of maturity and emotional health, especially in sexual matters. Therefore full restoration to pastoral ministry requires the professional judgment of the church.

A requirement of therapeutic evaluation and/or treatment may be utilized in combination with any of the six levels of response as listed above. This requirement should be clearly communicated and monitored as appropriate over time.

A requirement of payment for restitution of the victim(s) by the offending pastor may be made as a condition of the rehabilitation process and possible return to the clergy roster.

The bishop may limit the ministry of the offending pastor during the rehabilitation process and may appoint a trained supervisor to monitor the limited ministerial functions.

Evaluation and/or treatment should be carried out by therapists specially qualified to deal with sexual offenses and sensitive to issues of professional ethics. A qualified therapist should be selected by the offending pastor from a list provided by the bishop. Assistance will be made available for the spouse and the family. Possible reinstatement of the pastor on the clergy roster shall be dependent upon the therapist, supervisor, bishop and members of the committe on discipline concluding that the pastor is sufficently capable of effective ministry again.

Those agencies of the church responsible for clergy records shall be notified of the disciplinary actions of the committee on discipline so that no offending pastor may move to another synod without notice to that synod and his/her potential employees. In the case of misconduct determined to be 'major,' information on the nature of the misconduct and the actions of rehabilitation shall be given to those persons responsible for the call process in synods where the pastor is being considered for call and to the call committees of those congregations who are considering the pastor for call.

Once a pastor has been suspended or removed from the practice of the pastoral office, the matter of restoration is not merely an issue of absolution or forgiveness. The person is forgiven but the question of whether he/she is qualified for the office of pastor must be assessed in the more public grounds of the church.

Responses to the victim(s):

The bishop shall respond to the victim(s) of the misconduct by the offending pastor with sensitivity and care. An appropriate pastor or lay leader shall be named and offered to the victim(s) early in the process to serve as advocate and support, interpreter of the process, and pastoral presence.

A list of qualified therapists shall be provided to the victim(s) to be utilized at their choice. While this does not imply financial responsibility on the part of the synod, the Synod Council may offer financial support for this purpose. The committee on discipline may direct the offending pastor to make restitution to cover these expenses as a condition of restoration to office.

Where there are multiple victims identified, an opportunity should be made for these persons to meet together throughout the process.

Response to the congregation or agency:

The bishop and a representative of the committee on discipline shall meet with the congregation or agency board and communicate the results of the hearing process with special attention to the disciplinary action taken and its implications.

The bishop shall, in conjunction with the congregation or agency board, notify each member of the congregation or agency in writing of the particulars of the charges, their resolution and action taken by the committee on discipline.

The bishop or Synod Council shall make available a trained resource person who can assist the congregation or agency in whatever ways necessary to address their concerns so as to bring healing to their brokenness.

Footnotes

1. In dealing with an allegation of sexual misconduct the special consultation committee, in addition to the requirements listed in 19.15.05 of the ELCA Constitution (see footnote 5 below), shall, as much as possible, be made up of equal numbers of men and women. The members serving for special consultation from the consultation committee shall be appointed by the Synod Council or the synod executive committee for each separate consultation. Training in the special concerns of sexual contact should be provided for members of the special consultation committee to prepare them for their task.

2. In the event that a complaint involves allegations of sexual contact with a minor, the bishop and/or special consultation committee shall:

1. immediately report the suspicion of child sexual abuse to the state Child Protective Service or other appropriate legal agency.
2. proceed with the church's investigation process as outlined in this document.

If charges are filed involving criminal acts against a minor or adult, and the offending pastor is prosecuted, two members of the special consultation committee may be assigned to monitor the trial proceedings and report regularly to the consultation committee.

If the offending pastor is convicted in court of criminal charges against a minor or adult and the conviction is upheld, the special consultation committee should recommend to the committee on discipline permanent removal of the pastor from the clergy roster.

Acquittal of criminal charges shall not be understood to nullify any complaint brought to the bishop and/or committee on discipline. The church's process shall proceed seeking to determine whether unethical conduct ocurred on the part of the pastor against whom the complaint is brought.

3. If the complainant does not choose to pursue a formal, written complaint with the synod, the bishop and/or the special consultation committee, the special consultation committee may continue the investigation if there appears to be sufficient additional evidence that ethical misconduct occurred such that there is concern for the well-being of others in the church.

4. The accused pastor shall not engage in any pastoral duties or have contact with persons in the congregation or agency where he/she is serving except as is necessary to prepare a formal response to the complaint.

5. DISCIPLINARY ACTION, ELCA CONSTITUTION AND BYLAWS (19.15.10–05)

Consultation and Discipline

There shall be set forth in the bylaws a process of discipline governing ordained ministers, officers, the editor of the church periodical, associates in minsistry, congregations, and members of congregations. Such process shall assure due process and due protection for the accused, other parties, and this church. Since synods have responsibility for admittance of persons into the ordained ministry of this church or onto other rosters of this church and have oversight of pastoral/congregational relationships, the disciplinary process shall be a responsibility of the synod on behalf of this church and jointly with it.

The procedures for further consultation, investigation, and discipline set forth in the bylaws shall be the exclusive means of resolving all matters pertaining to the discipline of congregations of this church. Neither this church nor a synod of this church shall institute legal proceeding in which conduct described in provision 19.016.01. is the basis of a request for relief consisting of suspension of that congregation from the rights and privileges of a congregation of this church or removal of that congregation from the roll of congregations of this church. A congregation of this church shall not institute legal proceedings against this church or a synod of this church seeking injunctive or other relief against the imposition or enforcement of any disciplinary action against that congregation.

As used in this constitution and bylaws, due process means the right to be given specific written notice of the charges against any person or entity of this church, the right to testify in person or remain silent (at the election of the accused), the right to call witnesses and introduce documentary evidence concerning the pending charges, the right to confront and cross-examine all witnesses in support of such charges, the right to a public hearing at the request of the person or entity charged, and the right to be treated with fundamental procedural fairness. Any violation of these rights shall be grounds for reversal of an unfavorable finding and the right to a new hearing.

It is the intent of this church that all matters of discipline should be resolved internally to the greatest extent possible. It is the policy of this church not to resort to the civil courts of this land until all internal procedures and appeals have been exhausted, except for emergency situations involving a significant imminent risk of physical injury or severe loss or damage to property.

Ordained Ministers

19.15.01. Ordained ministers shall be subject to discipline for:

a. preaching and teaching in conflict with the faith confessed by this church;
b. conduct incompatible with the character of the ministerial office;
c. willfully disregarding or violating the functions and standards established by this church for the office of Word and Sacrament; or
d. willfully disregarding the provisions of the constitution or bylaws of this church.

19.15.02. The disciplinary actions which may be imposed are:

a. private censure and admonition by the bishop of the synod;
b. suspension from the office and functions of the ordained ministry in this church for a designated period or until there is satisfactory evidence of repentance and amendment; or
c. removal from the ordained ministry of this church, except in the case of discipline for willfully disregarding provisions of the constitution and bylaws of this church, other than 19.15.01 a., b., and c.

19.15.03. Charges against an ordained minister which could lead to discipline must be specific and in writing, subscribed to by the accuser(s), and be made by one or more of the following:

a. at least two-thirds of the members of the congregation's council, submitted to the synodical bishop;
b. at least one-third of the voting members of the congregation, submitted to the synodical bishop;
c. at least two-thirds of the members of the governing body to which the ordained minister, if not a parish pastor, is accountable, submitted to the synodical bishop;
d. at least 10 ordained ministers of the synod on whose roster the accused ordained minister is listed, submitted to the synodical bishop; or
e. the synodical bishop.

19.15.04. When there are indications that a cause for discipline exists, efforts shall be made by the bishop of the synod to resolve the situation by consultation; and if those efforts fail, the synod then shall activate the procedures for further consultation, investigation, and discipline, if warranted.

19.15.05. A consultation committee and a committee on discipline, both of which shall be standing committees of the synod, shall be utilized. The bishop of the synod shall be a member of the consultation committee ex officio except in instances when the bishop brings charges against an ordained minister. The bishop shall not be a member of the committee on discipline. The following procedure shall be employed:

a. There shall be a consultation committee consisting of 12 persons of whom five shall be ordained ministers, who shall each be elected by the synod assembly for a term of six years without consecutive re-election. From this committee the Synod Council, or a committee authorized by the council to make the selection, shall appoint five persons (three ordained ministers and two laypersons) to serve as a special consultation committee to consider the dispute. The special consultation committee shall meet with the accused and the accuser(s) in an effort to resolve the resolve the issue(s). If as a result of the consultation the charges are withdrawn, no further proceedings shall be required. If the charges are not withdrawn, the special consultation committee shall:

1. in the case of charges that do not anticipate disciplinary action submit a report in writing to the bishop of the synod which sets forth the charges and the action or actions recommended by the special consultation committee; or

2. in the case of charges that may result in disciplinary action, refer the charges in writing to the synodical committee on discipline for a hearing.

b. In the case of charges which do not anticipate disciplinary action, the bishop shall convey the recommendations of the special consultation committee to the parties. If either party does not accept the recommendations, that party may appeal the matter to the Synod Council, whose decisions shall be final.

c. There shall be a committee on discipline which shall be composed of 12 persons, of whom six (three ordained ministers and three laypersons) shall be the standing committee of the synod elected by the Synod Assembly for a term of six years each without consecutive reelection, and of whom six (three ordained ministers and three laypersons) shall be appointed by the Executive committee of the Church Council for the specific case. These six persons, appointed by the Executive Committee of 21 persons elected by the Churchwide Assembly for a term of six years each without consecutive reelection, to serve as needed in any of the synods of this church. The accused shall have the privilege of selecting two of the six who are to be appointed from the pool of 21. Each biennium the Synod Council shall designate the chair of the synodical committee on discipline from among the members of the committee on discipline elected by the Synod Assembly.

When a specific case arises, the chairperson of the committee on discipline shall advise the vice-president of this church of the need for the appointment of six persons from the churchwide committee to serve with the synodical committee. The vice-president, as chair of the Church Council, shall then bring the matter to the Executive Committee of the Church Council for the selection of the six persons panel.

In each specific case that may result in discipline, the synodical committee, as thus constituted, shall, within 45 days after receipt of the charges, meet with the ordained minister and the accuser(s) and render its judgment. If the charges are sustained, the committee shall impose the discipline appropriate to the case. Written notice of the date, time, and place of the hearing and a copy of the charges shall be delivered to the accused ordained minister and to the accuser(s) at least 20 days prior to the date of the hearing. At the hearing, the accuser(s) may present evidence in support of the charges and thereafter the ordained minister shall be entitled to present evidence. The accused and the accuser(s), or other person acting on behalf of either of them, shall be entitled to question the other party or any of the witnesses appearing on behalf of other party. A verbatim record shall be made by a stenographer or by tape recording of the hearing.

d. The decision of the committee on discipline shall be final unless, within 30 days, the accused ordained minister shall appeal the case to the Committee on Appeals. The decision of the Committee on Appeals shall be final.

e. If in the course of the proceedings, it should become apparent that the pastoral office cannot be conducted effectively in the parish being served by the ordained minister due to local conditions, the bishop of the synod may temporarily suspend the pastor from service in the parish without prejudice and with pay provided through a joint churchwide/synod fund and with housing provided by the congregation.

Education and Prevention

Education and awareness of self for the pastor and the congregation are key elements in the prevention of sexual misconduct. To be effective in preventing sexual misconduct, education and in-service training must be a priority for the church.

Synod Policy for Pastors:

Pastoral education needs to emphasize training concerning pastoral intimacy; including the trust which parishioners place in their pastors at times of vulnerability and the issues in the personal life of the pastor which place him/her at risk to behave inappropiately. This education should include knowledge of ethical guidelines and standards, and training in personal emotional health care for the pastor.

E1. Pastors who do any in-depth counseling of psychological issues are encouraged to receive qualified consultation/clinical supervision at the rate of one hour for each 8 to 10 hours of counseling performed. It may be permissible to charge a fee for counseling persons who are not members of the congregation, the proceeds helping to pay for qualified supervision. It is recommended that no more than 8 to 10 hours per week of counseling be provided by the congregation-based pastor unless he/she is a specialist. No more than four one-hour sessions with any one person are recommended unless the pastor is under supervision. In consultation/ supervision, the factors which put a pastor at risk to behave inappropriately should be clearly and openly discussed. Situations involving domestic violence, rape, sexual abuse, and child molestation should be counseled only under supervision and then to a limited degree. These are best referred as soon as possible to a specialist by the pastor.

E2. The guidelines and requirements of the American Association of Pastoral Counselors (AAPC), 9508A Lee Highway, Fairfax, VA, 22031, should be followed by those doing pastoral counseling as their major area of ministry. All counseling in the AAPC policy is done under clinical supervision.

E3. Synods cannot be expected to begin the process for all pastors of education in the complex area of relationships and the need to protect both pastor and parishioner. Colleges and seminaries preparing full-time church workers need to help the professional churchworker become open to self-examination, outside consultation and supervision.

Synod Policy For Congregations:

Congregations should adopt policies which show their concern for their health and that of their pastors. To properly prepare a congregation in using its leadership wisely, synod resources and leadership may be of great influence. They are able to provide training for congregations and councils in congregational and pastoral health. Congregational policies may be encouraged in the following ways:

F1. In the call process, the synodical staff may encourage the congregation to include in its self-study time an assessment of its expectations and policies for leadership.

F2. In the call process, recommendations may be made to budget funds for clergy care, consultation, counseling resources and education.

F3. Lay training conferences may be encouraged in individual congregations or jointly among several congregations.

F4. Pastors and professional leaders may be encouraged to ask for and use congregational support.

F5. The Division for Outreach of the ELCA may encourage support systems for pastors as a part of the budget for new congregations/missions.

Some issues to be addressed in the training of congregations include:

G1. The concept of safe boundaries within which pastors need to function. (see page 149, E1)

G2. Establishing clear and realistic expectations for leaders; i.e., their workloads, skills, etc.

G3. Establishing and training a pastor/staff support committee to support and facilitate mutual ministry.

G4. Establishing other kinds of support groups within the congregation or in the community as a personal resource for the pastor. Such groups need insightful persons who can be honest and compassionate.

Education and Support Opportunities:

Professional training, peer support and consultation:

Parish pastors often feel isolated, victimized by circumstances, personally unsupported and/or lacking professional options. Under stress they may be particularly at risk to the temptation of violating the professional role. Sensitive persons function best when a trusting atmosphere allows the expression of feelings and the stresses which prompt such feelings. Ongoing training which bridges the personal and professional areas of life and allows for intellectual care, emotional nuture and supportive relationships can contribute to a more positive outlook and a greater sense of control over one's life, destiny and vocational direction.

Many training opportunities on a local, synodical, or ecumenical level are available and include:

H1. Workshops, seminars, Lutheran and ecumenical programs which are on issues such as: counseling, alcohol and drug abuse, parenting, adolescence, child and adult abuse, marriage, family life, sexuality, conflict management for family and congregation, aging, adult life stages, self-care practices in ministry, and how to refer.

H2. Support groups among pastors which are intentionally planned and regular in their meetings. These may be created with peers in cluster areas. Sharing personal needs should be encouraged. Discussion of denominational business and programmatic issues at the expense of personal issues should be discouraged. Such groups may wish to use skilled facilitators to keep things on track, especially at first. One or more participants may wish to receive training in group leadership. Topics relevant to human needs may also be used to encourage sharing but the focus on personal emotional needs should not diminish.

H3. Pastoral mentoring programs are a creative innovation which can be encouraged on a formal basis. Bishops or other appropriate leaders may select a group of experienced mature pastors to be available as mentors to one or more less experienced pastors. The recipient may spend at least two hours per month with the mentor reviewing his/her schedule, sermons (taped), counseling, and self-care practices. Certified Pastoral Counselors are usually well-equipped to provide consulting services of this type. The synod's Consultation to Clergy is an available resource.

H4. Individual consultation or clinical supervision are easily arranged in most areas with competent trained professionals who have an understanding and acceptance of Christian ministry. Supervision is a recommended method for reducing the factors which place the pastor in risky situations and help the pastor learn ways to reduce stress in situations of pastoral intimacy. It is appropriate to use continuing education funds for this purpose. Congregational budgeting for supervision helps the congregation become a partner with the pastor in enhancing his/her ministry toward them. Lists of highly qualified professional counselors for supervision are available through the American Association of Pastoral Counselors, the bishop, clinical Pastoral Education supervisors, pastoral counseling centers, and the like. For pastors in isolated areas consultation resources can be made available at cluster meetings, pastors' conferences and synodical conventions.

H5. Small group consultation or clinical supervision groups, similar to the above, can be arranged more frequently due to sharing of costs with peers. One advantage may be in the wider range of situations presented for discussion by more participants.

H6. Referral is a vital subject to be learned. Appropriate referral is pastoral care. Knowledge of the limits of one's ability and time is a strength in ministry. The pastor's professional role and personal life are usually enhanced when his/her role is one of pastoral care, concern and spiritual nourishment while in-depth counseling is handled by an outside professional with whom the pastor is familiar. How to refer in a helpful way is a learned skill appreciated by most laypeople.

The pastor's care:

I1. Personal, marital, and family counseling are nearly always profound experiences. They enhance ministry and reduce the likelihood of problems among church professionals. Those in ministry need to be encouraged to seek counseling to enhance self-awareness. This is a form of self-care and is also professionally beneficial. Emotional awareness on the part of anyone doing counseling helps protect the counselee by keeping the personal struggles of the pastor apart from the counseling process and thereby fostering objectivity.

I2. Individual Confession and Forgiveness has been the church's instrument of healing and renewal throughout its history. Its decline in recent generations has proven to be a loss in the spiritual and emotional life of Christians. Lutheran theology and tradtion are richly supportive of this practice. The spiritual confessor is trained to listen. The confessor helps the person move toward a repentance which is a change of direction or behavior. Pastors, too, need to have confessors. The confessor may advise and refer the pastor to specialized treatment as part of absolution. Absolution then becomes a specific and personal experience of grace and affirmation. Absolution is not to be given cheaply or easily without genuine efforts to change. The practice of spiritual confesson is nuturing and prevents serious problems when used correctly and regularly.

Continuing education resources:

J1. As support for education and prevention, we encourage the use of existing resources such as: Lutheran Social Service of Washington, Lutheran Family Service of Oregon, Lutheran Counseling

Network, Luther Child Center, The Center for Prevention of Sexual and Domestic Violence, The Lutheran Institute for Theological Education, Consultation to Clergy, northwest theological training programs, pastoral and professional leaders' conferences, workshops at conventions and conferences, marriage and family enrichment programs and retreats, enrichment program emanating from pastoral counseling centers, and Growth in Ministry.

J2. The establishment of congregationally based Clinical Pastoral Education (CPE) throughout the region (in consultation with ACPE) is encouraged. Institution based CPE programs may also be used by the pastor. Clergy may be encouraged to participate, not as a punitive measure nor as a reactive step when personal conflicts and problems arise, but to enhance growth and professionalism. One or more quarters of training taken early in ministry (or at any time in one's professional life) are encouraged. Funding for congregationally based CPE needs to be explored. CPE supervisors in the region should be contacted regarding their availability for such innovative aproaches. A list of CPE supervisors can be obtained through Consultation to Clergy.

J3. The use of training programs, consultants, and centers related to the American Association of Pastoral Counselors (AAPC) is encouraged. These often exist in smaller cities as well as larger ones. They are ecumenical in sponsorship and constituency. Pastoral counseling is one of the fastest growing branches of the mental health profession. Training and supervision by the AAPC will lead to the establishment of credentials for pastoral counseling. The 'Pastoral Affiliate' status in AAPC is designed for the congregational pastor and provide a collegial and supportive professional organization for those interested in counseling.

Many training programs through AAPC and other counseling disciplines are linked to university-based graduate degree programs. Grants are often available to help finance the training.

Clergy and other church professionals sometimes feel undertrained in certain areas of their work. It is the desire of the Northwest Washington Synod that our seminaries, as they attempt to broaden training in pastoral ministry, continue to prepare pastors for human interaction. The synod urges the seminaries to plan their curriculum so that persons are prepared for the risks of service in a stressful, pressured and progressively secularized society.

Notes

EPIGRAPH

Margaret Atwood, *The Handmaid's Tale* (New York: Ballantine Books, 1985), 173-174.

PREFACE

1. Paxton Hibben, *Henry Ward Beecher: An American Portrait* (New York: The Press of the Readers Club, 1927,1942), 188-89.
2. *Ibid.*, 202.
3. Karen Lebacqz, *Professional Ethics—Power and Paradox* (Nashville: Abingdon Press, 1985), 128.

1. THE FIRST CHURCH OF NEWBURG

1. "District" refers to the regional structure of local churches that belong to this denomination. This District, made up of over 100 churches, maintains an office and staff of three ministers (an executive and two associates), who carry responsibility for administration of the regional church. An extensive committee structure made up of clergy and laity decides policy matters.

2. THE REVEREND DR. PETER DONOVAN

Epigraph: John D. MacDonald, *One More Sunday* (New York: Ballantine Books, 1984), 219.
1. The net increase in membership during Dr. Donovan's four-year tenure was just over 100. Average Sunday attendance increased by nearly 100 to about 250 his first year; peaked at over 340 in 1982; and decreased to about 250 his last year. An unusual number of new members recruited by Donovan were women of all ages. Many were revolving-door members, there and gone within a year.
2. A clergyperson who does not have standing and authorization from the District cannot be hired by a local church in the District.

3. THE WOMEN'S STORIES

Epigraphs: John D. MacDonald, *One More Sunday* (New York: Ballantine Books, 1984), 393, 216.

1. The issue of single pastors dating someone from their congregation is complicated. If Pete Donovan had genuinely been interested in pursuing a relationship with Joan Preston, he could have done so ethically. First they could have chosen to give up their pastor/parishioner relationship in order to pursue a romantic relationship possibly leading to marriage. He could then have made this new relationship known to the leadership of First Church in order to keep everything above board and open. This would have allowed their relationship to develop within the public eye, which would have minimized the occasion for unfounded rumor. Single pastors have to realize that they cannot have both a personal, intimate relationship and a professional, pastoral one with the same person. They have to choose.

   This also raises the question of the pastor's relationship to his or her partner in an already established relationship. Who pastors the pastor's partner? I would argue that the pastor cannot effectively play this role with his or her partner. It is important for the partner who desires a pastoral relationship to seek out someone other than his or her partner, the pastor, for this resource.

2. The exception to this situation occurs when the pastor is female and the parishioner is male. Here his power of gender may supersede her power of the pastoral role. A layman, because of the power of gender, size, and strength, may sexually coerce or force a clergywoman. This occasion of assault is not something the clergywoman could necessarily prevent.

4. THE CHURCH'S RESPONSE: "HEALING THE WOUND LIGHTLY"

1. There is another type of minister who engages in sexual activity with those whom they serve. I refer to this type as "the wanderer." At the time of the sexual activity with a parishioner, this minister is not functioning well personally or professionally. Conflict, inadequacy, and anxiety may well characterize this pastor's personal and professional relationships. He or she has difficulty maintaining boundaries in relationships, and attempts to meet private needs in public arenas. The use of physical touch or affection as a means of controlling an interaction is common and employed frequently, with no regard for its possible negative impact on the recipient. This clergyperson takes little care of himself or herself and is easily overwhelmed by stress. Thus the opportunity to "fall" into a relationship with someone who is emotionally vulnerable and who holds the pastor in total positive regard to the point of adoration is a temptation to which the wanderer responds. He or she is attracted to the adoration and vulnerability and is at great risk to become emotionally and sexually involved with a parishioner or counselee.

2. The ministry committee of the District is the body within the regional structure of the denomination which is responsible for authorization of clergy. They examine and approve candidates for ordination; they accept transfers of clergy into the District from other districts. They are delegated the task of dealing with any charge of misconduct that might be brought about an individual clergyperson. A pastor has to be in good standing with this committee in order to serve a local church. Ultimately, this committee was called upon to deal with Pete Donovan.

3. The position of District minister in this denomination is somewhat comparable to a bishop in a more hierarchical denominational structure. The District minister is the executive and administrator of the District. He or she is responsible for the well-being of the member churches and clergy of the District. Although Rev. Maxwell Kelley did not have the power or authority of a bishop simply to remove Donovan from his position, he did have the moral weight of his office to see that the established process was brought to bear.

4. This lack of specificity whenever clergy ethics are delineated by denominations is quite different from other professional groups. The other helping professions have very clear and unambiguous statements as to the inappropriateness of sexual contact with clients. Their ethical comprehension of these matters is far more advanced than that of the church. The Ethical Principles for the American Psychological Association are the most comprehensive: "Psychologists make every effort to avoid dual relationships that could impair their professional judgment or increase the risk of exploitation. Examples of such dual relationships include, but are not limited to research with and treatment of employees, students, supervisees, close friends, or relatives. Sexual intimacies with clients are unethical. . . . Psychologists do not exploit their professional relationships with clients, supervisees, students, employees, or research participants sexually or otherwise. Psychologists do not condone or engage in sexual harassment. Sexual harassment is defined as deliberate or repeated comments, gestures, or physical contacts of a sexual nature that are unwanted by the recipient." ("Ethical Principles of Psychologists," *American Psychologist 36* (June 1981): 636–37.

5. Mediation presupposes a conflict between two parties of equal power who need help in negotiating a resolution of issues. For example, a local church dispute between the board of trustees and the finance committee over use of funds for renovation of the church.

6. Withdrawing First Church from the denomination was very possible within this particular denominational polity, which values local church autonomy above all else. Donovan believed that so long as First Church members did not have information about him, he could retain the political clout to sway First Church to leave the denomination and retain him as their pastor. How serious he was about this action was never clear, but he nonetheless used the threat to intimidate the District. Had he attempted this route, he would have divided the congregation and he and his supporters would have tried to withdraw from the denomination, taking the assets and church facilities with them. The District wanted to avoid this split if at all possible. Even an unsuccessful attempt by Donovan would have wreaked still more havoc within the membership.

7. However, it was never clear why the District had so little confidence in its own power to prevent First Church leaving the denomination. The District never accurately assessed its own resources, not the least of which were the facts that the District held the mortgage on First Church and that most of the church's long-standing members would have rallied to maintain the denominational affiliation.

8. Don Ivy later explained that his reference to "verbiage" was an incomplete quote (he had not intended to discount the women), and that the second statement was true: Based on what they knew, most of the members *did* hold Donovan in high regard.

9. "When bad practices are well entrenched, efforts on the part of concerned individuals to halt them by publicizing their destructive effects are more likely to arouse derogation than sympathy for the victims." Albert Bandura, *Agression: A Social Learning Analysis* (Englewood Cliffs, NJ: Prentice-Hall, Inc., 1973), 214. This was what worried me about speaking out for the women at this meeting.

5. HOW COULD THIS HAPPEN HERE?

1. The question addressed here is not how did Donovan become an offender. For more information on offenders, See M. Walker and S. Brody, Eds., *Sexual Assault: The Victim and the Rapist* (Lexington, MA: Lexington Books, 1976) and N. Groth with J. Birnbaum, *Men Who Rape* (New York: Plenum Press, 1979). The question discussed here is what happens when a local church intersects with an offending pastor.

2. In the early eighties, no denominational body was adequately prepared to deal with this problem or to use their current policies and procedures to respond.

3. This varies according to the polity of the denomination. For example, a strong congregational polity (church governance being centered at the local church level rather than in a regional or national hierarchy) minimizes the denominational involvement in matters requiring discipline. It assumes that such things should and will be dealt with at the local church level. Yet this polity also provides for credentialing of clergy at the regional level. Examination for fitness for ministry is handled by a regional committee, which then approves ordination and standing at this level. Nonetheless, the regional church's authority in matters of discipline is ambiguous. In an episcopal polity, the responsibility for discipline lies with the bishop at the regional level. The discipline process is much less ambiguous.

4. This was the response of the Assemblies of God to Rev. Jim Bakker and his PTL television ministry.

5. Karen Lebacqz, *Professional Ethics: Power and Paradox* (Nashville: Abingdon Press, 1985), 114–15.

6. On the issue of power derived from a contract in contrast to "unfettered authority," see *Ibid.*, 126.

7. *Ibid.*, 111.

8. *Ibid.*, 121.

9. David K. Switzer, *Pastor, Preacher, Person: Developing a Pastoral Ministry in Depth* (Nashville: Abingdon Press, 1979), 17, as quoted in Lebacqz, *Professional Ethics*, 113.

10. This is also not to say that the laity are powerless vis-à-vis the pastor. Especially in congregational polity, the laity at the local church level retain decision-making power and authority (e.g., the power to hire and fire). In this case, they could have collectively used that power to stop Donovan much earlier. However, there remains the dynamic of laity deferring to the pastor's leadership role, which was exploited particularly well by Donovan. In addition, the individual layperson, particularly in a time of personal crisis or turmoil, does not see herself as carrying authority vis-à-vis her pastor; it is rather the opposite.

11. It has always been something of a puzzle how Donovan managed the number of simultaneous involvements *and* got any work done. He was a very competent administrator.

12. "Attribution of blame to victims is still another expedient that can be used for self-assuaging purposes. In this process, aggressors see themselves as essentially persons of goodwill who are forced into punitive actions by villainous opponents. Victims are condemned for bringing the suffering on themselves either by their character defects or by their witless and provocative behavior." Albert Bandura, *Aggression: A Social Learning Analysis* (Englewood Cliffs, NJ: Prentice-Hall, 1973), 214.

13. See Policy and Procedures section in the Appendix.

6. DOING JUSTICE AND MERCY

Epigraph: Willard Gaylin, *The Killing of Bonnie Garland* (New York: Simon and Schuster, 1982), 17.

1. The process of arriving at the truth of a matter requires that anyone against whom such serious allegations are made have the right to fair treatment and due process. That opportunity was offered to Donovan and he refused it. I also offered him the opportunity to be interviewed for this book. I received no response to three efforts to contact him for this purpose.

2. Ellen Thompson Luepker and Carol Retsch-Bogart found that most of the victims of therapist abuse whom they saw in treatment expressed shame and guilt about the experience. Many of them connected these feelings to a sense of responsibility for having "seduced" their therapist. This was not the case for the victims of Pete Donovan. None of them felt responsible for seducing him, even though several did initially agree to the relationship. Their shame related more to their embarrassment about the intimate nature of their involvement and the difficulty of sharing this information with others, and their gullibility. Ellen Thompson Luepker and Carol Retsch-Bogart, "Group Treatment for Clients Who Have Been Sexually Involved with Their Psychotherapists," in *Sexual Exploitation by Health Professionals*, Anne Burgess, ed., (New York: Praeger Medical Press, 1986).

3. *Ibid.*

4. See Shirley Feldman-Summers and Gwendolyn Jones, "Psychological Impacts of Sexual Contact Between Therapists or Other Health Care Practitioners and Their Clients," *Journal of Consulting and Clinical Psychology* (1984): 105–61.

5. See Feldman-Summers and Jones.

6. Jim Bakker is reported to have said to Jessica Hahn: "When you serve the shepherd, you are serving the sheep."

7. This is the principle of moral agency put forth by many ethicists including Beverly Harrison in *Making the Connections* (Boston: Beacon Press, 1985) 8–12.

8. *Ibid.*, 12–15.

9. *Ibid.*, 15–21. See also Carter Heyward, *The Redemption of God: A Theology of Mutual Relation* (Washington, DC: University Press of America, 1982); Carol Gilligan, *In a Different Voice* (Cambridge, MA: Harvard University Press, 1982); Margaret Farley, *Personal Commitments* (San Francisco: Harper & Row, 1986).

10. The ethical framework I suggest here is shaped primarily by feminist ethical theory and practice as it is rooted in Jewish and Christian traditions. These contexts are especially important in application to this particular situation.

11. Carol Gilligan argues that women tend to place highest value on maintaining relationship with others, and that this shapes their moral interaction with them. This was certainly true for the women victims: Their relationships with the church and with individuals in the church, as well as with Donovan himself, were of primary importance and fueled their determination to seek restoration of the brokenness. Gilligan might argue, and I would concur, that faced with the same situation, many men would simply walk away. These women could not do that.

12. Right-relation describes a norm of relationship based upon love and justice. It is *agape* which moves us to seek union with others and with God; justice requires that this union be shaped by mutuality, safety, trust, choice, responsibility, and respect for bodily integrity (see Marie Fortune, *Sexual Violence: The Unmentionable Sin*, [New York: Pilgrim Press, 1983], 81–87). The norm of right-relation applies regardless of the nature of relationship (i.e., employer-employee, parent-child, pastor-parishioner, lover-lover). In each of these types of relationships, additional factors will apply because of the nature of the relationship.

13. Bandura goes on to link lack of acknowledgment with victim-blaming: "When blame is convincingly ascribed, victims may eventually come to believe the degrading characterizations they hear about themselves. . . . Negative attribution by itself may not be too persuasive, but it is usually accompanied by maltreatment that produces self-confirming evidence of the victims defects of badness. Vindicated inhumanity is thus more likely to instill self-contempt in victims than if it does not justify itself." Albert Bandura, *Aggression: A Social Learning Analysis* (Englewood Cliffs, NJ: Prentice-Hall, 1973), 214.

14. A process of adjudication also can provide equity and fairness for the offender in judging the veracity of the allegations.

15. Note Policy and Procedures provisions in the Appendix.

16. Willard Gaylin, *The Killing of Bonnie Garland* (New York: Simon and Schuster, 1982), 336.

17. Jody Alieson, from the title of her poem, "Doing Least Harm."

18. See Geoffrey Blodgett, "Woodhull, Victoria Claflin," in *Notable American Women 1607–1950*, Edward James, ed. (Cambridge, MA: The Belknap Press of Harvard University Press, 1971), 652–55.

19. This is the basic premise of Charles Rassieur's book, *The Problem Clergymen Don't Talk ABout*, (Philadelphia: Westminster Press, 1976). His case material is drawn exclusively from male pastors who fear seduction or who have been "seduced." While he does assert the professional nature of the pastoral relationship and the need to prevent sexual activity from entering it, he never addresses the pastor's problem of misuse of power and authority to gain sexual access to a parishioner or client.

20. My assertion is true for situations of male clergy vis-à-vis female or male parishioners or clients and for female clergy vis-à-vis female parishioners or clients. The position of female clergy vis-à-vis male parishioners or clients differs. In such relationships, the female pastor's gender makes her vulnerable to male parishioners or clients because the power differences based on

gender supersede those based on role. In this patriarchal society, a female is always vulnerable to male violence, regardless of the roles of either. Rev. Katie Simpson could have been assaulted by a male parishioner as readily as by Donovan, a male clergy peer.

21. Bandura, *Aggression*, 214.
22. Karen Lebacqz, *Professional Ethics—Power and Paradox* (Nashville: Abingdon Press, 1985), 128.
23. Those still wanting to be convinced that patriarchy is a source of oppression in the church should see works by Mary Daly, Rosemary Ruether, Beverly Harrison, Margaret Farley, Jacqlyn Grant, Katie Cannon, Elizabeth Fiorenza, and others.
24. Matilda Josyln Gage, *Woman, Church and State* (Watertown, MA: Persephone Press, 1980; original edition, 1893), 208, 285.
25. See Fortune, *Sexual Violence*, 208–11. Forgiveness on the part of victims of violation becomes an option if some form of justice has been done on their behalf. The preceding discussion of vindication best summarizes the experience necessary for a victim to be able to forgive.
26. Gaylin, *Bonnie Garland*, 330.

EPILOGUE

1. Paxton Hibben, *Henry Ward Beecher: An American Portrait* (New York: The Press of the Readers Club, 1927, 1942), 200.

Index